Praise for How Do I Reach My True Destiny?

"AWESOME! This is a must read for all. The spirit in which this book is written is neither threatening nor critical; however, it is feedback for self-development at its best. In addition, Vince provides several step-by-step approaches and prescriptions for success."

—James C. Tolliver, vice president of sales, Sara Lee Food & Beverage

Vince has provided an inspirational and educational guide, which will benefit all. I was particularly moved in realizing that freedom is truly achieved when we can appreciate "*What happens to us is not as important as how we respond to what happens to us.*" This lesson, I am trying to teach my two sons at this very moment in their life. Thanks for giving me a tool to do so.

—Mark Norman, director of operations, Johnson & Wales University

This book is destined to become a favorite. It is very practical and can be understood quickly by everyone who wants to succeed in life.

—**Frank E. Gadsden**, school administrator, Charlotte Mecklenburg School System

How Do I Reach My True Destiny?

How Do I Reach My True Destiny?

✦

9 Principles for Authentic Living and Maximizing Your Potential

Vincent T. Williams

iUniverse, Inc.

New York Lincoln Shanghai

How Do I Reach My True Destiny?
9 Principles for Authentic Living and Maximizing Your Potential

iUniverse books may be ordered through booksellers or by contacting:

iUniverse
2021 Pine Lake Road, Suite 100
Lincoln, NE 68512
www.iuniverse.com
1-800-Authors (1-800-288-4677)

ISBN: 978-0-595-42679-9 (pbk)
ISBN: 978-0-595-87277-0 (cloth)
ISBN: 978-0-595-87009-7 (ebk)

Printed in the United States of America

*By believing passionately in something
that still does not exist, we create it.
The nonexistent is whatever
we have not sufficiently desired.*
—Nikos Kazantzakis

20th Century Greek writer and philosopher

This book is dedicated in loving memory of:

My mother, Birdie Mae Williams,
for driving me to achieve and for guiding
me in developing core values of faith in God,
love of family, and compassion for others;

Prentice Williams,
my brother and best friend, church member, and role model,
who admonished me daily to TCB *take care of business*;

Reverend Henry Williams,
my uncle, who taught me to dream and have a vision, and
that second place is the first loser; and, most important,
when life's burdens get too heavy to carry, *let go and let God*;

David Allen,
for allowing me to apprentice under his leadership.
I will always look for him in the winner's circle;

David Christopher Stephens,
my mental gym and analytical scuba-diving partner,
who engaged me in deep, deep conversations,
gave me daily encouragement, and
believed in my dream.

Contents

Acknowledgments

First and foremost, I acknowledge and thank God the Father of the earth, moon, and all of the cosmos, for establishing Himself within me, and for providing the vision and insight to write this book.

This body of work is the result of a lifetime of learning and personal development. It is also the collective participation of many mentors, teachers, supporters, advisors, friends, and family. This work has served as both a journal and a mentoring tool for my life. We are the product of our life experiences, as well as the community of people who have contributed to our lives, as we journey to our ultimate destiny.

Our success is owed to the input and involvement of many cohorts. No achievement in life is without the help of many known and unknown individuals who have impacted our lives. Here are just a few who made this work possible.

Roberto Anderson has been my devoted friend and brother. Barbara Busy, a dear friend and contributing editor, assisted me in organizing my initial thoughts. Mike Whitehead and Ken Samuelson were major contributors in my development as a socially responsible, confident and strategic thinker. Dawn Butler was great friend and supporter during the final stages of the book. Greg Morris, my uncle, has served as a role model and life time mentor. Colin Quashie used his artistic talents to provide images to my vision. Images are extremely empowering to ideas. Leslie Ware merits special mention for her extraordinary generosity. My friend and ghost writer, a true lab assistant, she scoured over each paragraph repeatedly. She was instrumental in helping me articulate many of the concepts in the book. My brother-in-law Roosevelt

Harris and friends Greg Bryant, Sporty Jeralds, Columbus Copeland, Mike Kearney, and Kevin Huff, along with many other special friends who encouraged me on this project.

Author's Note

Within every human being resides a dream.
For many, this dream has been realized.
But for most, their dreams are trapped
within, never to be attained, or even pursued.
—Vincent T. Williams

To the aspiring dreamers and achievers, there is a divine, foreordained greatness in each of us. Stay true to the desires of your heart. Never, ever abandon your dreams. May you touch your own light and discover your true destiny.

To the accomplished, you have acquired much in the form of wealth, position, material, or academics, yet, if you have not achieved that which fulfills your spirit, may this work encourage you to retreat and pursue the desires of your heart.

To my acclaimed contemporaries and colleagues: teachers, preachers, coaches, and speakers—those who empower the world—you are the true models of leadership. May you continue to inspire those who seek to achieve what God has ordained for their life.

Preface

What if after living your whole life, you discover you've lived the wrong one? Living a life of authenticity means evolving consciously and conducting an ongoing investigation of truth; the truth about who you really are, and where you are in life. Understand that life circumstances are but learning experiences. As you subject yourself to self-examination, listen to your thoughts, and look at your choices, you will benefit from each lesson and maximize your potential.

Personal growth is a journey, not a destination. There is no designated point of arrival. It is a never-ending process. In this work, I will take you on part of that journey. By revealing the power of wisdom and several principles commonly practiced by great achievers, I will show you what is possible in your own life. God has deliberately designed all of us with individual significance. When you discover this gift of distinction, buried deep within, you will experience a wonderful transformation. Your old way of thinking will be lost, and a more expansive and productive perspective will open you up to new potential.

Personal-development and self-help books often present one of two extremes. They are either overly religious, thereby crippling us with the belief that God will take care of everything if we just have faith, or they lend themselves to the philosophy that we alone, completely control our own destiny. Conversely, in this text I articulate that reaching your true destiny is a balanced incorporation of God's grace and individual choices; God's will and freewill.

This book will help all who read it to realize that self-actualization, *the art of being true to oneself,* is challenging, yet an essential philosophy for authentic living. My purpose is to empower one's ability to achieve without boundaries; to assist individuals of all backgrounds with leveraging the power of the human mind to reach their most desired dreams. I will share an idea many of us have embraced, but probably never questioned. Reaching your true destiny requires a mental transformation from the model posed by Western society, which suggests financial and material gain determines success, to living by the principle of a passion-directed life. My mantra is *Follow Your Dream*.

Who am I to be your guide on this journey? Well, I am no Oxford guru on success. However, I will teach you the value of failure as an achievement principle. Neither am I a *name it and claim it* spiritual evangelist, though you will find I am a man of faith. I, too, am a work in progress and, in my own journey, have formed my values from the tenets of the Good Book. I am an individual who, in my desire to successfully pursue my own dreams, became exposed to a number of highly effective tools of empowerment. I wrote this book because I knew writing it would be helpful to me first, and also, to anyone who would read it. In particular, it would be of great benefit to my nieces and nephews. These common sense principles can be applied by anyone, from the homeless, to the corporate executive.

As a child growing up in the southernmost region of Alabama, my family was unfamiliar with many of the strategies and mind-sets of high achievers. My mother was a woman of both faith and trust in God; she was ahead of her time. She was a compassionate leader with great drive and vision. She once told me when I was a teenager, "I am the head of this family, but I lead from behind. I never get in front of your father." Her proclamation sent my mind whirling like a spinning top on a marble floor. Many women of today might find themselves challenged by her beliefs. My father is a tall man that many women still consider strikingly handsome. He is well respected in the community, and at the mature age of seventy-eight, still has the endurance and work ethic of a farmyard mule. Work is his hobby. He has always been the nucleus of his and my mother's family. A gamesman, he enjoys hunting wild animals and trained us well in the sport of survival, which included gardening. My parents provided a good home and raised us with excellent core values. We were taught to love our family, work hard, and trust in God; not merely to have faith in God, but to *trust* in God. Understand, faith is theory, but trust is practical application. To further elaborate, faith is a noun, but trust is a verb. If you trust and believe, you should then take confident action in pursuit of your dreams.

My parents surprised even themselves with their accomplishments. However, being relatively unexposed, common people, they believed that, to do great things, you must come from a historically great and accomplished background. They did not understand that *potential* resides within all of us. Any one of us is quite capable of great achievement. I remember my mother telling me I could be the president of the United States. On one hand, my parents taught me to believe I could be whatever I desired, but in reality, my parents were unable to support an uncommon career path or a path unfamiliar to them.

There was a contradiction between my parents' words and their actions. Though my parents encouraged us to be high achievers, their actions were the result of a well-meaning parental act of caution and protection. Our social background created a culture, which caused my parents to feel they needed to protect me from the disappointment of a failed attempt at what appeared to them as a *pipe dream*. Our environment had confined their thought patterns to a narrow imagination of life possibilities. My chosen paths were usually *outside the box* of my upbringing. Consequently, my goals were viewed by my parents and siblings as overly ambitious or egotistical pursuits. Therefore, many opportunities were lost. It is my goal to share principles and strategies that will sustain those who find themselves among similar social mind-sets.

SOMETIMES FAMILY AND FRIENDS ARE UNABLE TO SUPPORT AN UNCOMMON CAREER PATH OR A PATH UNFAMILIAR TO THEM.

For most of my life, I have been intrigued by human behavior. I have often wondered, when we don't get the results we desire, why we don't change our behavior. How do we change our behavior? I have also questioned why one person succeeds and another fails. Why some make millions and others live a life of poverty? How do we produce the results we want?

Comprehension of these mysteries required an exploration of the vast pool of experience related to human behavior. In my daily walk, I have spent many hours observing, talking with, and even had the privilege to work with champions and peak performers. It has been said, *Success leaves clues* and I have found many of those *clues*. For as long as I can remember, I have, with great fascination, examined and analyzed the success secrets and behavior models left by those who exemplified a sense of discovered destiny in their achievements. Through my investigation, I identified nine key success principles to assist you in maximizing your potential—living on purpose, responsibility, self control, consistency, discipline, failure, mental toughness, leadership, and inner peace.

WHEN WE ARE NOT GETTING THE RESULTS WE DESIRE, WHY DON'T WE CHANGE OUR BEHAVIOR?

As I began applying these strategies in my life, I was empowered with the confidence and courage to pursue my most desired dreams. I now share these principles to empower professionals, business owners, athletes, ministers, principals, schoolteachers, and everyday working class individuals. Wherever you might find yourself, if you learn and adopt these principles, you will essentially possess the tools required to proficiently and quickly adjust your approach to life, just as a skillful mechanic can tune or repair your vehicle. Your challenge is to obtain enough mental leverage to act on your newly acquired knowledge.

We struggle with the mental decision required to change our behavior, even when we know we have been introduced to a more efficient method of doing things. Let me ask you a couple of questions. Do you believe you are a relatively intelligent individual? Have you attended a workshop, college course, business conference, or any type of personal-development seminar? Did you learn something you really, truly knew was valuable, but never actually applied what you learned?

YOUR CHALLENGE IS TO OBTAIN ENOUGH MENTAL LEVERAGE TO ACT ON YOUR NEWLY ACQUIRED KNOWLEDGE.

How is it that an intelligent person, like you or me, could learn something and know it is valuable, but still not use it? One reason this occurs is our opposition to change. We are naturally reluctant to deviate from our normal routine or comfort zone. This happens, largely, because we have not acquired the wisdom and mind-set to take action. After a wide-ranging level of growth and development, I have found that knowledge without wisdom is just information. And that wisdom is the appropriate use of information. I have also found the cliché "*knowledge is power*" to be just that, a cliché. It is important to understand that knowledge and wisdom together are merely *potential* power. Please be clear, only one thing gives you power—*action!*

Knowing what to do is not enough. We must take *action*. We actually have to *do the work!* This is where most of us fall down. We simply cannot gain enough leverage to consistently do what must be done. To be successful, we must *will* ourselves to take action on a daily basis to reach our goals. I have personally taken on the wisdom to harness the power of *action*. In the Good Book, I am reminded, "Even so faith, if it hath not works, is dead, being alone" (James 2:17 KJV).

ONLY ONE THING GIVES YOU POWER— ACTION ...

When taking action, it is critically important that you have the right tools. I am sure you can remember attempting a simple task, such as tightening a screw or changing a tire, only to discover you did not have the correct tool. So, you called a neighbor for help. No luck. You drove to the hardware store. No luck. Finally, the clerk at the hardware store, knew who carried the tool you needed and directed you there. In the meantime, what should have taken only a few minutes took hours to successfully complete. Our lives are similar. Some of us live our entire life using old-aged; ineffective, commonplace methods, attempting to gain clarity of our life's direction. Others travel, what seems, the world over before discovering their true destiny. We know this approach as *trial and error.* What if we could save ourselves most of this *wasted* time of trial and error? What if you possessed some of the most effective tools and then took *action* to use them?

This book is one of those vital tools. It will help make possible the results you desire in your professional and personal life. You have an inherent gift specific to you. Perhaps you have seen a glimpse of it for a brief moment, only to have it return to its place of hibernation. The problem is the methods you are using are unable to draw out your gifts and harness their power. The intent of this work is not to benefit you alone. It is my wish that you share this book with your family and friends. I am certain if you adopt the principles and apply the strategies outlined, you will find personal fulfillment, while reaching your true destiny.

What is your destiny?

We often claim to be authors of our own destiny. Yet, we spend most of our time as passengers on the journey of life, instead of *driving the bus*. As humans, we share the aspiration to live happy, productive lives, but happiness is a condition we often find too complicated to grasp. Happiness is not a discrete, nor a sustainable state. We have the same individual perceptions about happiness as we do about beauty, justice, and goodness. Many of us believe if we could just fulfill our dreams and passions in life, we would be happy. Yet, to achieve true emotional satisfaction and purpose, it is necessary to obtain the *courage* to pursue your dreams. It is then you will discover your true destiny.

Destiny is defined as the purpose or future, as arranged or foreordained by the Divine or by God. Based on this definition, one may ask why am I attempting to tell you how to reach your true destiny? The answer to this question can be found in the pages that follow. Our destiny is inherent—we were born with it. But to fulfill it, you have to do something! To reach our true destiny, we must first release the self-imposed limitations. It's a fact. Let me ask you a question. Who keeps us down most of the time? We do, of course. We are the cause of our own mediocrity. It is based on our beliefs about who we are, and who we can become. Let me say that again. It is based on our beliefs about who we are and who we can become. When we change our belief system and pursue our dreams with passion and determination, we will ultimately realize our true destiny.

WHEN WE CHANGE OUR BELIEF SYSTEM AND PURSUE OUR DREAMS WITH PASSION AND DETERMINATION, WE WILL ULTIMATELY REALIZE OUR TRUE DESTINY!

We all have dreams. Some of us dream of competing in the Olympics and bringing home the gold. Some of us dream of being the president of our own corporation, while others dream of connecting with a soul mate and building a wonderful family. Many people are satisfied with a day's work and catching the game on the sports channel before passing out on the couch. To imagine what you want to become or do in life is wonderful. Unfortunately, after experiencing some of life's harsh disappointments and unknowingly sharing our dreams with dream-killers who discourage and impede our progress, we lower our beliefs and expectations (*self-efficacy*) of who we can become. To rejuvenate those expectations and obtain the results we desire, we have to learn to use new patterns of thinking and behaving. It means changing our perspective.

I do not profess to share any philosophy or ideology you have never heard before. In fact, you probably have, if you have been paying attention. I do not guarantee any overnight success or breakthroughs. Success is hard work! Neither do I offer some philosophical *Think Positive* self-talk. My purpose here is to add value to your life by highlighting how our environmental and cultural traditions can teach us behaviors that can create mental impediments. In adding value to others lives, I am left with a great feeling of self-significance. I want to remind you, if your current plan is not producing the results you desire in your life, you must try something different! It is a well-known fact, if you continue to do things the same way; you are going to get the same results. The first step in changing your outcomes is changing your outlook; the second is changing your behavior. *Real sustainable change does not happen in a moment. It is a process. But the decision to change happens in an instant.*

In our effort to understand our own behavior, it is important to know that our human nature is to inventory more of our negative life experiences than our positive life experiences. The memory of our unpleasant situations far exceeds our recollection of our pleasant ones. As a result, our adverse experiences become the dominant character of our perspective, shaping and forming our personal belief system. In the classic games of competition such as championship tournaments, the loser remembers feelings of disappointment much longer than the winners celebrate or remember their feelings of adulation and victory. You will learn we are psychologically at war with our collective experiences. Every day, inside our minds, we are in a mental battle with the historical influence of our past relationships, both personal, and professional. We are at war with our past and present social environments, and these experiences play a major role in shaping our *thought life.* We must win the battle in our minds. It is extremely important you take control of your thought life.

One of the vulnerabilities of our thought life is its subjection to fear and conformity. Our thoughts are greatly persuaded by fear of failure and disappointment. We struggle with the courage to march to our own beat. Most of us lack the courage to step out of our comfort zone to follow what is in our heart. Consequently, we conform by copying the masses. We behave like everyone else without knowing why, and without having any idea what the people we are modeling are doing, or where they are going. Hip Hop music mogul Russell Simmons says it best in the title of his new book, "*Do You.*" In short, be tough enough to be you. We must tap into the power of our inner self. Be yourself or you may try to be someone else. However, you will find that everyone else is already taken. We tend to go with what is perceived as the norm, or popular notion. In the book of Romans we are instructed, "… be not conformed of this world; but be ye transformed by the renewing of your mind …" (Romans 12:2 KJV). When you manage your thought life, you gain better control of your decisions. When you change your thoughts, you change your life.

WHEN YOU CHANGE YOUR THOUGHTS, YOU CHANGE YOUR LIFE.

Your thoughts are your own; no one else controls them. You control your own thinking and your goal is to lend your thoughts to things that have value and meaning to you. To do this, you must have a sense of certainty about who you are and what you want to accomplish in your life. How do you obtain that certainty? You have to *do the* self-reflective *work* to gain clarity. In order to achieve clarity about your goals and dreams, you have to first, see it within. You have to become laser beam sharp about where your passions reside. You will have to conduct a thorough search and examination of yourself to clearly identify your passions and your gifts. Clarity of ones desires and talents is no guarantee one will reach their true destiny. However, without clear direction, reaching your full potential is impossible. *Inner Work = Self-Examination = Identification of Your Passion = Clarity = Certainty = True Destiny*

A common trait I found among high achievers is their insatiable appetite for new knowledge. Champions, peak performers, and precision thinkers, constantly invest in themselves. They read. They employ consultants. They attend seminars. They will move heaven and earth to obtain the information they believe will move them forward in their professional and personal lives. Too often we spend money on *things* instead of investing in ourselves. You have to take inventory of your personal tools and investments (books, tapes, classes, seminars), and determine what is going to increase your value. Every day we step over dollars, trying to save pennies, because we do not realize the importance of investing in ourselves. If you *act* on what you have learned, the returns will far outweigh any investment you have ever made. So, do not be afraid to invest in yourself.

A COMMON TRAIT AMONG HIGH ACHIEVERS IS THEIR INSATIABLE APPETITE FOR NEW KNOWLEDGE.

This book can be one of those investments. Here you will find specific principles to help facilitate your journey to reach your true destiny. Of course, reading the text is easy, but the words on the page cannot apply the principles. To gain a return on your investment, you will have to make a concerted and disciplined effort to consistently practice the principles. Obtaining personal achievement in one's individual life causes an inner peace and joy. You will find when you have personal fulfillment; you will become a better producer in all areas of your life.

TODAY—this very moment—begins the rest of your life. So, decide *right now* to choose the outcome of your life. Be aware, life will throw you what seems like unendurable challenges. *The pain of your journey at times will cause you to question your destiny.* Do not lose your belief in your goals. On occasions certain conditions and situations will be uncomfortable, but you must respect the journey. *Your trials and triumphs create your testimony.* You cannot escape the difficulties of life, whether you do your personal best or just rise daily and produce the bare minimum needed for survival. There is no place to hide. Will pain still stop by to visit you late at night in the form of an unbearable migraine? Will the pale rider called death unexpectedly show up at the home of a relative or loved one? Will life introduce you to the pain and frustration of falling short in achieving some of your most desired goals? Will you experience some *cut-your-heart-out* disappointment in your marriage or other closely connected companionship? Of course you will. The key is deciding how you will respond. I suggest you grab life, and demand what is yours. The success principles in this book are for those who are committed to doing more with their lives, and those who desire to positively impact the people around them. Mark this day as the day you made the commitment to change your life—*Get in the game! Do not stand on the sidelines. Get in the game! Follow your dreams, and discover your true destiny.*

LIVING ON PURPOSE

✦

*PURPOSE: INTENT—PROPOSED AS AN AIM
FOR ONESELF; THE REASON FOR WHICH
SOMETHING EXISTS.*

There is a point in life where most of us come to a crossroad. Somewhere between thirty-five and fifty-five years of age, the infamous mid-life crisis appears. There is an unrest that visits us, and we begin to ask questions like, "Is this all there is?" As we ponder deeper, the unrest begins to feel like a void, a sense of emptiness. We feel as if something is missing, but we can't quite put our finger on it. Our life seems to lack meaning. Gradually, we come to the realization that our value system to pursue the American Dream—which includes the accumulation of status symbols and material rewards—isn't doing it for us.

This occurs mostly, because we confuse money with success. We also confuse goals with purpose. For example, it may be your *goal* to purchase a Mercedes by age thirty, but what is your *purpose*? It is important to understand that there is a difference between setting goals and having a purpose. Your purpose is the big picture—it transcends your goals. A goal is something specific that you want to accomplish. The purpose is why you want to accomplish it. You may have several goals within your purpose. Your goals are the steps you take along the journey to realize your purpose.

YOUR PURPOSE IS THE BIG PICTURE; IT TRANSCENDS YOUR GOALS.

To clarify your purpose, you have to ask yourself a series of questions: Why do I want to do this? Why do I dream of doing it? Harriet "Dr. Ball" Ball, a mentor and close friend, is a divinely gifted teacher and facilitator. Harriett is often referred to as Dr. Ball because of the remarkably amazing results she produces with students labeled at risk or unreachable. After a visit from Dr. Ball, students feel like they have experienced an educational and attitudinal revival or healing. Parents see remarkable differences in their child's academics. For twenty years, Dr. Ball worked as an educator and counselor in the public school systems in San Antonio, Austin, and Houston, Texas. She was often mocked and criticized for her non-traditional methods as a school-teacher.

She is now well-known for her techniques and incredible results as a national speaker and facilitator. In the course of a week, requests for seminars and workshops may take her to Washington D.C., New York, Detroit, Chicago, and New Orleans. She has been profiled on *60 Minutes*, *CBS News* and the *Oprah Winfrey Show*. When I first met Dr. Ball in the airport, suffering with chronic back and leg pain, she could barely walk. I asked her why she was traveling in such a condition. She said, "It's my *passion.* I have to do it. I am passionate about children who are labeled unreachable, and I want to prove that the labels are wrong and inappropriate." Simply stated, Dr. Ball is living on purpose.

Dr. Ball has found something that fills her with enthusiasm and excitement every day. She has the purpose and passion, which are the motivations necessary for life to have meaning. Her soul has been granted the fulfillment most of us seek. Her *goal* is to perform workshops for underachieving students and seminars to train educators in modern methods for transferring knowledge. Everyday she is fueled by an adrenaline surge and tremendous fervor, which allows her to achieve her *purpose*—to make sure no student is left behind. Her life has excitement and meaning.

When you have a fire in your belly to do something, you can do the impossible. So many people simply go through the motions every day, caught up in life's routines that often become boring. If you are experiencing this meaningless merry-go-round in life, do not fret. There is an abundant life for you when you begin to live your life on purpose.

You must first identify your talents to discover your purpose. You may not believe you have an inherent talent, but you do—it is your gift. By using your gift to the fullest, you will positively impact your own life and the lives of those around you. You will recognize your gift when you identify your *passion*. What do you love to do? What gets you excited? What gives you great fulfillment and satisfaction? It can be anything: cooking, math, writing, sports, gardening, art or singing. Maybe you love helping people, or maybe you enjoy solving complex problems. If you can identify, what you love to do, you are on your way to discovering your purpose.

So, if you love kids, your purpose might be to help children succeed, or to simply be a wonderful parent. If you love to draw or paint, your purpose may be to bridge the gap of race relations through art. If you have a great analytical mind and enjoy business challenges, your purpose could be to use your gifts in the world of commerce to help the federal government build a better business model or to help a corporation prosper by restructuring their organization.

When you do what you love, and love what you do, you will find true fulfillment. Mother Hale of New York had a passion for children. Throughout her life she worked tirelessly to give unwanted children the love and support they so desperately needed. Her life's work was truly a labor of love. Hale House stands today, as a testament to her passion. I know you can think of many examples of men and women who have found tremendous joy in their work, because it provided them with a feeling of *purpose*. Be determined to make your life an *experience of intentional pursuits.*

Once you have identified your passion, you will be able to clarify your purpose. Here are five fundamental elements essential in discovering your purpose:

- Purpose Statement

- Alignment

- Determination

- Humility

- Visualization

Purpose Statement: A ***Purpose Statement*** states clearly and simply your *reason for being.* For example, my purpose is to bridge the gap of race relations through art. Whether you own your business, or simply would like to set your own purpose in motion, I suggest you start by writing a *Purpose Statement* instead of a *Mission Statement.* Often, company executives and individuals with well-meaning intentions, fashion some grandiose statement about their mission, which no one remembers. Keep it short and simple, one sentence. Devise a powerful statement (*Our Purpose* or *My Purpose*), which you and/or your employees can use every day; it will add meaning to your life and theirs.

Alignment: *Align* your purpose with your natural ability—with your passion. Use your natural ability as the vehicle to achieve your goals. We have all been gifted with natural talents. Discovering what they are is part of the game of life. For most of us, our work is not aligned with what we do best. Our values and our actions may be at *cross-purposes* or opposed to each other. These mixed messages can cause internal conflict and uncertainty. When you align your purpose with your passion, you will enjoy peace of mind and a wonderful sense of life.

Determination: *Being **determined*** is a trait of perseverance. Perseverance is the power to endure failure and difficulty again and again. It is motivated by faith in a purpose. Be determined every day to stay true to your purpose, no matter what—family, friends, companions, and especially unexpected setbacks. Determination is vital. It is a mind-set that will add power to your drive, even if no one else believes in your pursuit. Many of us lose our direction or focus because we are easily distracted and influenced by other people. Without knowing, we are being sidetracked and persuaded by our environment. The daily activities and conversations we are involved in with friends and associates, often neither encourage nor support our goals or purpose. In most cases, our activities are contradictory to our aim. You may also lose focus when you are engaged in an incompatible personal relationship. Your partners' inability to see or believe in your goals can pull you down emotionally and cause you to deviate from your objective. Accordingly, a loss of direction or focus happens when one has no purpose in life. Once you have chosen your direction, remain focused, and use determination to bolster your pursuit.

DETERMINATION WILL ADD POWER TO REINFORCE YOUR DRIVE, EVEN IF NO ONE ELSE BELIEVES IN YOUR PURSUIT.

Humility: *Humility* can be a useful tool for staying grounded. It may also serve as a daily prescription to prevent the development of an egoist. Egoism is a dangerous psychological state. It can create a lethal and toxic flaw in our character and decision-making abilities. An inflated ego also will cause you to lose your focus. Focus is the most central element in the achievement of anything we pursue. It's impossible to fail at anything you are focused on. In 1985, Harry Belafonte recruited music genius Quincy Jones to bring together the largest group of singing superstars ever to be assembled in the same studio at one time. Imagine for a moment, Lionel Richie, Whitney Houston, Bono, Madonna, Diana Ross, Cindy Lauper, Willie Nelson, Michael Jackson, Stevie Wonder, Bob Dylan, Ray Charles and many other musical icons all in the same studio. These artists were brought together for the making of *We Are the World,* the world-famous song created to raise awareness and money to provide relief for starving Africans. Quincy Jones knew and envisioned how challenging and destructive multiple egos could be to the project. In his foresight, as he sent copies of the instrumentals to the interested musicians, he included a letter that stated they should *"check their ego at the door."* He also posted his admonishment outside the studio door. Quincy was able to maintain an atmosphere of openness and modesty with everyone. The project was a historic success. *We Are the World* won Grammys in 1985 for Song of the Year and Record of the Year. As your sense of accomplishment grows, so will your confidence, and confidence can breed ego. So, remember the importance of humility in your daily life.

AN EGOTISTIC CONDITION IS A DANGEROUS PSYCHOLOGICAL STATE— IT CAN CREATE A LETHAL AND TOXIC FLAW IN OUR CHARACTER AND IN OUR DECISION-MAKING.

Visualization: "Where there is no vision, the people will perish ..." (Proverbs 29:18 KJV). Vision is the ability to see the ending, before the beginning. You have to picture the outcome of the achievement of your goal. It is important to know what this accomplishment does for you, prior to your pursuit. What is the result of achieving this goal? What is the benefit to you? It is important to gain some sense of what it feels like to have achieved the goal. This is what drives you in your purpose.

Visualization is an in-depth imaginative process of picturing yourself doing what you really desire to do. It is a recognized and proven success tool. Many high-level achievers employ this method to increase the likelihood of success in achieving their goals. If you desire to learn advanced visualization techniques, search the Internet for coaches and books. They will guide and coach you through the process of how to employ advanced visualization techniques.

Visualization is the employment of virtual reality. You are picturing your success. As you picture the outcomes of your purpose, be specific. The more specific your picture, the more obvious the obstacles become. My friend, Ken Samuelson describes it this way: "The ability to dream, see the obstacles and transform them into strategies is the *distinguishing feature* of people who transform the world rather than just living their lives responding to the world." There are certain fundamental obstacles that will impede you—time, money, knowledge, support, resources, and emotional opposition. But if you can visualize how to overcome these obstacles, you will learn to harness the power of the opposition by determining the solution long before you come face to face with the obstacle.

> *THE ABILITY TO DREAM, TO SEE THE OBSTACLES, AND TRANSFORM THEM INTO STRATEGIES, IS THE DISTINGUISHING FEATURE OF PEOPLE WHO TRANSFORM THE WORLD RATHER THAN JUST LIVING THEIR LIVES RESPONDING TO THE WORLD.*

It is up to you to decide what you want to experience in life. You make choices every day. You may not realize it, but you are designing your life with each moment, through the choices you make, the priorities you set, the job you have, the friends you surround yourself with, and the beliefs you hold. All of these choices *custom design* your life. When you choose fulfillment over perceived security, your values become your guiding principles. Choose your career path by the passion you have for the work, and not by its income opportunity. When you choose the path of fulfillment, you are choosing a *passion-directed* life. In other words, when your life is passion directed, you are designing a life that reflects the core of who you really are.

Having a passion-directed life has a positive ripple effect. Your work is excellent because it is personally fulfilling and reflects you and your passion. The inner man/woman within us desires true authentication. For instance, if your current career is that of an architect, but your passion is to be a fireman, a music sound producer or an airplane pilot, *you will not possess true fulfillment until the passion of your spirit is fulfilled.* When we pursue a path we delight in, the rewards are boundless.

You will discover that your mind is at ease because you find enjoyment and fulfillment in your activities. A healthy state of mind will cause you to excel in all areas of your life—self, career, family, and community. Being balanced gives life new meaning. You will no longer just move from one day to the next. You will look forward to each new day because it offers you the opportunity to use your unique abilities.

YOU ARE CREATING YOUR LIFE WITH EACH MOMENT THROUGH THE CHOICES YOU MAKE.

Following your dreams and passions in life takes courage and sacrifice. Are you committed to do that? It requires being brutally honest with yourself. What will you do with this knowledge? Fulfilling your purpose may necessitate changing careers, furthering your education, or something else that causes you to leave your *comfort zone.* Are you ready to take action? The life you choose will not always be easy. Therefore, you must develop an inner conviction and belief that you will and can do whatever it takes to achieve your dreams. "Be strong and of good courage …" (Joshua 1:6 KJV)

Decide today to find your passion in life, and get busy fulfilling it. Your work is vitally important in fulfilling your purpose. Most of us spend more than 50 percent of our daily hours working. Obviously financial remuneration is one reason we work. Yet to be fulfilled, we must enjoy what we do and use our innate abilities creatively. Regardless of your occupation, it has value. So, resolve in your mind that you will bring all of who you are to your work and ennoble it with a style that is distinctly yours. Spend some time discovering where your passions lie and give your life *purpose.*

IT TAKES COURAGE AND SELF-SACRIFICE TO FOLLOW YOUR DREAMS.

- **Employ the strategies below to help you cultivate the principle of Living on Purpose:**

Take a blank sheet of paper and write down the answers to these questions:

1. What do I really love to do?

2. What do most people say I am good at doing?

3. What would I do for free?

4. What do I really want to become?

From those answers, write your purpose statement. Make your work a labor of love, and all your achievements will be meaningful and satisfying.

RESPONSIBILITY

✦

RESPONSIBILITY: THE STATE OF BEING
OBLIGATED, RELIABLE,
AND DEPENDABLE, OR ACCOUNTABLE FOR
THE OUTCOME, MEDIOCRE OR FABULOUS.

In today's culture, senior management is quick to take credit or accept responsibility for achievement in a group effort. I believe we can agree the success the Chicago Bulls experienced in the 90s was a team effort. However, it is difficult to deny that Michael Jordan's work ethic and competitive leadership were responsible for his teammates' aggressive, *never-quit*, attitude, which won six championships. Yet, in many published articles, books, and nationally televised interviews, we have read or viewed the behind-the-scenes feud between nine-time NBA Championship coach Phil Jackson (formerly the Bulls' head coach), former vice president of operations, Jerry Kraus, and even the team owner, Jerry Reinsdorf, claiming responsibility for the team's outstanding success. It is human nature to desire the association with, or credit for, something done well.

Still, after more than nine years, no one among the executive leadership of the Bulls organization has accepted responsibility for the fallout and dismantlement of one of the greatest teams ever to compete on a professional level. Responsibility is about accountability. It is about holding yourself accountable for your successes and failures. Accountability is a personal admission of one's conduct and motives for taking a certain action. Remember sneaking out for a drive in dad's car, before you were licensed to drive? For the ladies, maybe it was getting caught wearing makeup before you had your parents' approval. Responsibility is not about accepting the consequences for getting caught. Instead, it is about the conversation you have with yourself—an honest admission of your motive. It does not matter whether your motive was a sincere effort to create a positive outcome or whether your choice came by your desire to impress others. The greatest opportunity for personal growth is holding yourself liable for your choices, and learning the lessons to make better decisions for future achievement.

We can change our lives for the better by mastering the principle of responsibility. Many people blame others or something outside themselves for their circumstances. We must take charge of our lives and be determined to cause our own good fortune. Another pitfall is to view successful people as the lucky ones, somehow predestined for greatness. No one can make it alone, but understand that every person who has achieved anything in life decided to take responsibility for making it happen.

EVERY PERSON WHO HAS ACHIEVED ANYTHING IN LIFE DECIDED TO TAKE RESPONSIBILITY FOR MAKING IT HAPPEN.

Nineteenth century poet Oliver Wendell Holmes, Sr. is famous for the quote *Making It Happen*, "Great is not in where we stand, but in what direction we are moving. We must sail sometimes with the wind and sometimes against it—but sail we must, and not drift nor lie at anchor." Know that you deserve to experience the joy of winning, and accept the responsibility for making your dreams come true. You are what you think you are! Remind yourself of your greatness every day, and step into the world of a truly successful person. You must dream big and realize that you can achieve your heart's deepest desire. Being responsible for those dreams involves acknowledging them ourselves. We have to continually affirm and confirm what we will accomplish, as if we already have; and in our mind we will begin laying out the plans needed to do so. Your *should-do's* must become your *must-do's*.

YOUR SHOULD-DO'S MUST BECOME YOUR MUST-DO'S.

I have highlighted three essential elements to employ in developing the concept of responsibility:

- **Time:** Start by taking responsibility for your time. According to Greek philosopher Theophrastus, "Time is the most valuable commodity a person has to spend." Notice where you are spending your time each day and devise a work schedule that is flexible enough for play. Pay close attention to those with whom you spend your time, including friends, and even your choice of companion. I am suggesting you become constructively selfish. There are moments in our pursuit that will require our undivided attention. These are significant short periods, necessitating a single-minded focus. Align yourself with friends, who can add value to your goals. It has been said, we are the sum of our five closest friends. Hence, we should choose friends or partners that add unto us in our journey. During one of his Sunday sermons, Rev. T. D. Jakes, stated, "If you are the go-to person in your circle, you probably have outgrown your circle." If your friends are not holding you accountable for your progress, then you should consider finding a new circle. One way to strengthen your support system is to develop an accountability group, a core group of like-minded goal-oriented individuals. The group should consist of four to ten people that will commit to meet once a month for four hours. You can agree to meet every other month or once a quarter, but never less than four hours. The purpose of the meeting is to hold you in report of your progress and to share obstacles the group may be able to assist one another with.

- **High expectations:** Setting high expectations for yourself will help you develop the principle of responsibility. The planning and pursuing of your goals are more important than actually achieving the goals themselves. The transformation and metamorphosis your mental state undergoes is a far greater reward. By setting big goals for yourself, you birth new possibilities for your future. We must believe we can succeed, because it is true. The world is filled with limitless possibilities. Our job is to decide what we want to experience and make it real. Remember, life will give only what we have the courage to demand.

- **Obstacles:** In the previous chapter, I pointed out the specific hurdles we will face in achieving our dreams. None of them are more challenging than our emotional opposition. At times, we will encounter those who will try to stand in our way and discourage us. These occurrences have been known to create mental conflict in the form of self-doubt. Here, we have to be careful not to pass the buck by believing that others have somehow kept us down. Instead, rejoice because those nay-sayers will fuel our motivation by creating what is called a *teachable moment.* Our success is bigger than us. It will inspire others—even our adversaries. By consciously practicing the principle of responsibility, your success will serve as a teachable moment for the skeptics, demonstrating the possibilities for their own life. Accept full responsibility for your choices, decisions, and failures. Learn from the experiences of your failures and press forward in your pursuit.

IT IS NOT IMPORTANT WHERE WE START IN LIFE.
IT IS HOW WE LIVE LIFE THAT COUNTS.

It is not important where we *start* in life. It is how we *live life* that counts. How did you impact and contribute to your community, church, or school? Maybe you grew up in a foster home, because your parents were deceased or addicted to drugs. Maybe your mother gave birth to you while in prison. Or maybe you grew up without knowing your father. We have no control over where we are born and the many circumstances of our upbringing. While our environment has a definite influence in our life, sometimes creating a major disadvantage; we must not live in the past. We must gaze, forever, toward the future. It is *now* that is real, and *we* control the choices we make. So, it is our responsibility to create the life we want.

Do not allow negative experiences to keep you from stepping out of your current reality. Free yourself from thoughts that are holding you hostage, confining you from being who you really are. You can alter your present condition by making a conscious commitment to take the driver's seat of your own life. It is well known that children of affluent families often feel they have to measure up to the success of their family and even follow the same path. If you are among those who have enjoyed the good fortune of wealth through inheritance, you may own to a double-edged sword. This imposed standard can be a source of identity conflict and feelings of inadequacy rooted in the belief that their parents' success is too great to follow. However, the truth about their achievement is just that, it's *their* accomplishments, not yours. No matter what our circumstances, we all have our own destiny. So, the questions you must ask yourself is, "*What path will I take?*" *What will be my legacy?* No one knows what the future holds, but everyone needs to plan for it. It is better to be prepared for an opportunity that never comes, than to be unprepared for one that does. Your future holds great promise. Making it real is your responsibility! So, chart your own course and set sail!

YOU CAN ALTER YOUR PRESENT CONDITION BY MAKING A CONSCIOUS COMMITMENT TO STEP INTO THE DRIVER'S SEAT.

• **Employ the strategies below to help you cultivate the principle of Responsibility:**

1. Identify realistic goals and tasks that can make a difference today.

2. Decide how you will contribute to others around you and in your community.

3. Outline a plan for achieving your goals, and dedicate time every day to work on them.

4. Volunteer to chair a project at church or in your community.

5. When you find yourself making excuses or blaming others for any failures or undesired results, determine what you could have done differently.

Share your experiences with others. By sharing, your success will have greater meaning and satisfaction.

SELF-CONTROL

✦

SELF-CONTROL: THE ABILITY TO MANAGE ONE'S EMOTIONS AND IMPULSES.

Road Rage is a prevailing event on our roadways today. Drivers yell, honk their horns, and give the proverbial finger. In several incidents people have even been murdered. Self-control, if exercised as a guiding principle, would make road rage and a few other embarrassing out-of-control moments non-existent. The amount of success and happiness we experience in life is directly related to our ability to effectively exercise restraint over our impulses, emotions, and desires. This is a critical and key principle of success. When I speak of success, I am referring to balance, balance between self, family, career, community interests, and spiritual communion.

Self-control is essential to providing the stability for great achievement. You must master the art of self-control, because it will help you develop the skill to balance your life. Mastering self-control will improve your ability to preside over your choices. Know, that you, and only you, are accountable for what you achieve or do not achieve, regardless of your starting point in life. Some of us truly have extremely difficult circumstances, but we must find a way to move forward. In many cases, if no one steps up to pursue a life of significance, an entire family can be cursed by a repetitive cycle of mediocrity and poverty, one generation after another. It only takes the commitment of one person to change the family's history. Strive to gain a level of discipline, which empowers you to think and act constructively. In the chapter of Proverbs, the *Good Book* tells us, "For as he thinketh in his heart, so is he" (Proverbs 23:7 KJV). What we actually produce in life is the direct result of our own thoughts. God is the greatest influential source in our lives. Second to his grace, our thoughts have the foremost influence on what we will do or become.

> *GOD IS THE GREATEST INFLUENTIAL SOURCE IN OUR LIVES,*
> *SECOND TO HIS GRACE, THE THOUGHTS WE THINK HAVE THE*
> *FOREMOST INFLUENCE ON WHAT WE WILL DO OR BECOME.*

Be determined to govern your thoughts by practicing intent conscious living. Living intently allows you to be more cognizant of your daily decisions. By being mindful of your thought patterns and choices, you bring better order and stability to your world. One of the primary benefits of having self-control is the ability to have command of your reactions as you deal with life challenges. There will always be situations you cannot foresee or control. However, by having a measure of self-control, you can intentionally decide to react in a constructive manner.

To develop better self-control, obtain clarity about what is really important to you in life. Determine what you want out of life and make definite plans to achieve your major goals. When you internalize your goals, they become an integral part of your beliefs and values. You develop greater awareness of your emotions and this enables your ability to better manage your response to others' opinions. Criticism and negative comments from others will no longer be followed by a negative reaction from you. Instead, a bigger picture will guide your thoughts and actions.

Furthermore, you must work to improve the mental ability to contain the impulses of your alter ego, which would otherwise sabotage your own success. It is okay when everything doesn't go your way. Without failures, setbacks, and disappointments there can be no growth. Throughout the history of mankind, we have progressed more as a society through failure than success. Celebrate others' triumphs over adversity, and use their achievements as inspiration for your own goals. Adapt and adopt success characteristics of champions and high-level achievers you know and admire. Your attitude when you lose or fail will determine how long it will be before you succeed.

LEVERAGE YOUR MIND POWER TO CHOOSE HOW YOU BEHAVE UNDER ANY CIRCUMSTANCE.

Practicing self-control improves your ability to live a balanced life. Making time for family is extremely important. What good does it do you to possess a million dollars without the time to enjoy it, or loved ones to share it with? Self-control includes having respect for your time. Use it wisely! By setting a daily and weekly agenda, you can predetermine how you will spend or allocate your time in pursuit of your individual goals. It is important to schedule time for family and friends, time to exercise, time to work, and time to be alone. Practicing the discipline of self-control will increase your ability to manage your urge to do other things that are contrary to your goals. Loss of focus will certainly cause you to fail at obtaining the success you seek. Your chief aim is to develop yourself to the fullest, to always offer your personal best. You can leverage the power of your mind to choose how you behave under *any circumstance,* by mastering the principle of self-control.

- **Employ the strategies below to help you cultivate the principle of Self-Control:**

  1. Obtain clarity in what's really important in your life. Write down the top five things you would like to accomplish over the next five years. Then write down the top three things you want to accomplish in the next three years.

  2. When something upsets you, stop to think about the consequences of your response. Always remember, your thoughts determine your actions and your actions determine your outcome.

  3. When your plan unexpectedly goes in the wrong direction, develop a mantra, such as, "It is okay when everything doesn't go my way," and repeat it often.

  4. Think positively about every setback and problem. Learn the lessons from those experiences.

CONSISTENCY

♦

CONSISTENCY: SUCCESSIVELY DEMONSTRATING RELIABLE AND UNIFORM RESULTS.

Hall of Fame baseball player Hank Aaron characterizes the success of committing to a firm and consistent work ethic. Mr. Aaron never had a 50-home-run season like some of the big hitters today. However, he consistently hit 20 or more home runs for twenty consecutive seasons. Hank Aaron displayed notable consistency in his play in the face of racial slurs, denial of basic human rights, and even daily death threats. Mr. Aarons' major league record of 755 career home runs, is being challenged for the first time in thirty years. This accomplishment demonstrates the example that a consistent work ethic can produce uncommon results.

Consistency is the one principle you will find the most challenging. I struggle every week to maintain a regular schedule for exercise. One week I may get to the gym five days, and the next, maybe only two days. It seems as if something always comes up which I consider to be more important at the time. Please be certain to understand, in each occurrence, I made a choice to give something else priority over exercise. Each decision you make is a personal *choice*. Once we start to see the results of our efforts, it fuels our desire for consistency in a particular goal or cause. Therefore, stay with your effort until you are able to see the first peak of results, and you will be inspired to achieve even better results.

Everyone has the ability to change their actions for a moment and produce a desirable result. People who lose weight by dieting prove this every day. However, to be truly successful, we must learn to bring consistency in our actions every day. Diets often do not work because, once the pounds are shed, the dieter returns to the same eating patterns he or she had before losing the weight. It works the same way in other areas of your life. A onetime shot will not produce long-lasting results. It's imperative that we work to develop consistency in our daily actions.

Being consistent in your actions will help you perform at a more productive level. "The race is not to the swift, nor the battle to the strong, neither yet bread to the wise, nor yet riches to men of understanding, nor favour to men of skill; but time and chance happeneth to them all" (Ecclesiastes 9:11 KJV). The prize of achievement is only obtained by those who press on. By consistently using our abilities to accomplish our goals, we will continue to improve. Consistency requires perseverance. Perseverance is a definite means to success, even if—and especially if—we experience setbacks. President John Calvin Coolidge declared; "Nothing in the world can take the place of perseverance. Talent will not; nothing is more common than unsuccessful men with talent. Genius will not; unrewarded genius is almost a proverb. Education will not; the world is full of educated derelicts. Persistence and determination alone are omnipotent."

YOUR ABILITY TO GET THINGS DONE WILL ELICIT CONFIDENCE AND TRUST FROM OTHERS.

By performing a task at a consistent level, you will develop a proficiency that others rely on, and you will create a demand for your work. Your capacity to get things done will elicit confidence and trust from others. Moreover, you will find it easier to acquire the help you need to complete the task. You will then be a person others admire because of your *sustained performance* and your desire for improvement. Mastering the art of consistency will create a footprint that sets you apart from those who work just the adequate amount to remain employed or those who work only when the feeling strikes them.

You must enjoy what you do in order to develop the consistency necessary for success. This is why it is critical to establish goals that are compatible with your talents and abilities. Your goals must excite and incite you, even when you are not in the *right frame of mind.* As the intensity of your desire grows to accomplish your aspiration, you will enthusiastically take the action necessary to move you closer to your purpose. Be determined to spend each day working on something meaningful to you. Consistency is a true winning practice. All successful people either have or developed a practice of working relentlessly on their goals. They consistently take the steps essential to attain the success they desire.

Most of us lack the discipline required to delay immediate gratification. Pause here for a moment to absorb this statement. In most cases, the achievement of any goal, large or small, requires some extended time and personal sacrifice. Success came to many well-known achievers, only after many years of financial agony and meager lifestyles. Some even found themselves homeless in their quest. Sure, like so many of us, they desired some of life's finer trappings. However, they enjoyed life and entertained themselves in the everyday pursuit and anticipation of their dream. More significantly, they possessed the discipline of delayed gratification.

Develop the mind-set to look at success as a long-term proposition. Commit yourself to sustaining your performance for as long as it takes to succeed. Even after you reach your objective, you will reach yet a higher goal because you have developed the habit of winning. You will become someone others can depend on to get the job done, and you will be splendidly rewarded for your efforts.

MOST PEOPLE LACK THE DISCIPLINE REQUIRED TO DELAY IMMEDIATE GRATIFICATION.

Realize the importance of developing the habit of consistency, and you definitely will succeed at attaining your desires. Champions expect to win because they know by consistently following the strategies of other champions; they will arrive at their goal. In his First Law of Motion, physicist Sir Isaac Newton stated, "A body in motion tends to remain in motion." I suggest you start your ball rolling, and it will pick up momentum with each passing day. As you get better at performing the tasks necessary to obtain your goals, you can win *big* if you move toward your dreams with consistency.

- **Employ the strategies below to help you cultivate the principle of Consistency:**

  1. Be true to yourself—make sure your goals are where your passions reside. It is much easier to maintain consistency when you enjoy what you are doing.

  2. Develop a plan to achieve your pursuit, and *stick to it.*

  3. Make sure you spend at least thirty minutes a day on your goals, no matter what.

  4. Develop some new habits to move you closer to achieving your goals: rise thirty minutes earlier to exercise; read the *Good Book*—read a self-development book every day and be consistent for thirty days. Medical studies show, routines becomes habits after thirty days.

DISCIPLINE

♦

*DISCIPLINE: THE WILL TO SUCCESSFULLY
FOCUS AND FOLLOW A STATE OF ORDER
BASED
ON SUBMISSION TO RULES OR A SYSTEMATIC
METHOD TO OBTAIN A CERTAIN RESULT.*

What better model for practicing discipline than the Olympian. Olympic athletes possess the utmost discipline with *delayed gratification*. For many athletes, it takes many years of arduous training and work before the medal is won. My friend Robert was born in Jamaica and raised in Canada. At a young age, he had big ideas about his future. Imagine for a moment growing up on the tiny island of Jamaica, dreaming of being the fastest man on the planet. Better yet, picture two individuals from totally different parts of the planet, connecting over similar ideals. Making this acquaintance would be life changing for both of us. It was three o'clock in the morning. I was checking my e-mail in the business center while cruising through the Caribbean on Carnival Cruise Line, when Olympic gold medalist Robert "Blastoff" Esmie walked into the center carrying a sandwich bag filled with a snack he was eating.

Being raised by a father who makes syrup from sugarcane he grows, I easily recognized his snack as chunks of peeled sugarcane. Knowing he would be surprised I could identify such an unusual snack, I sarcastically asked Robert why he had not offered to share his sugarcane. With a shocked look on his face and a bright smile, Robert responded in his Jamaican accent, "Yah mon, have sum." The sharing of the cane led to a discussion about our life experiences, which continued beyond daybreak. I asked Robert if he would tell me about his journey, but before he would tell me his story, he said, "I have something to show you." When we arrived to his cabin, he pulled out a beautiful mahogany wood jewelry box. He opened the box and there lie the Olympic gold medal. I was speechless, humbled by its significance. As I was standing there attempting to grasp the magnitude of his accomplishment, he removed the medal from the box and kindly placed it around my neck. He then instructed me to stand in the mirror, and say to myself, "Dreams do come true." This was an unexpected, but tremendously considerate act on his part to encourage me in my pursuit. It was an extremely empowering moment in my life, an affirmation of my belief in the power of *acting* on your dream.

After taking a few minutes to physically share his gold medal, Robert told me his story. He shared how he dreamed and trained his entire life, hoping to become the fastest man in the world. He continued to share how he dreamed and trained, and trained and dreamed day and night, night and day, for over ten years, hoping to qualify for the Olympics. Once he gained recognition by the authorities as a world-class runner, he continued to compete to obtain Olympic certification by the International Olympic Committee (IOC). After certification, he was observed for an additional four years by the IOC. He had to demonstrate a sustained superiority among other Olympic athletes.

In 1994, he won a gold medal in the 4x100m relay at the Commonwealth Games and did it again in the 1995 World Championships. After exhibiting a long-term dominance, he was selected to represent Canada. Once selected, he had to adjust to constant attention by the media, while being on the world's stage. Robert explained how he had to exercise discipline on every level—which included his associations, environment, and his mental toughness. His discipline also incorporated time management, requiring training four times a day, regulating his amount of sleep, and depriving himself of some things most people take for granted, such as not being able to eat his favorite foods, or spend time with his family, friends, or even his companion. Robert was not slated to run with the relay team at the 1996 Summer Olympics in Atlanta; he was an alternate. Can you envision getting that close to your dream and not being selected to actually run with the team? However, staying true to his dream, and maintaining his readiness, the night before the race, he replaced Carlton Chambers. Robert was a part of the Canadian 4x100m relay team, which beat the United States by almost half a second to establish itself as the best relay team in the world.

It is important to understand some goals may take years, or even an entire lifetime, and there will be many obstacles. Once you make up your mind to do something special in your life, please know you will encounter hardships and setbacks on your success journey. At times, it will take every ounce of your will to stand up after life has delivered a devastating blow. In September 1986, former heavyweight boxing champion Joe Frazier had eleven wins, all by knockout, with no losses. He was matched with a great slugger, Oscar Bonavena, in an incredible fight. Frazier was badly beaten, completely dominated, and knocked down twice. To all in attendance, he seemed bound to lose. He staggered back to his feet with a determined will, and the discipline to follow the steps of his rigorous training and preparation. He persevered and swept the next six rounds to win a unanimous decision. Joe Frazier's legacy is remembered by his ability to get back up after multiple knock-downs. Joe was inducted into the Boxing Hall of Fame in 1990.

Every person who has known great achievement has used the principle of discipline. Discipline involves developing the capacity to take charge of yourself by controlling your thoughts and actions. What happens to us is not as important as how we respond to what happens to us. We must learn to force ourselves to continually do those things that will move us closer to our ambitions in spite of the impediments we may encounter.

WHAT HAPPENS TO US IS NOT AS IMPORTANT AS HOW WE RESPOND TO WHAT HAPPENS TO US.

Professed friends will be the number one skeptics of your desire to build a better life, and they will explain why your goals are unattainable. Others who are jealous or envious may try to trip you up. Your adversaries will seek to bury you in your self-pity when things do not go as planned. And there are those well-meaning souls who do not want you to *get hurt* by failing in your endeavors. Yet, the biggest stumbling block is *you*! We constantly remind ourselves of all the reasons why it is impossible to reach those mega-dreams we desperately want to fulfill. So we don't even try, and if by chance we do, it is only a half-hearted attempt at best. It is vital that you take control of your life and focus your attention on those things that are positive and constructive. Self-discipline will enable you to quickly dismiss negative thoughts and replace them with empowering thoughts and ideas that, if acted upon, will propel you toward your objective.

When you lack mental toughness, your mind will show you several reasons why you are unable to accomplish your goals. It is during those times, you must dig deep within yourself to find the strength to move ahead in the pursuit of your goals.

By developing the capacity to be more disciplined, we dramatically increase our probability for success. You must understand that the principle of discipline can be mastered by anyone committed to improving his or her life. How do you do that? The answer is: the same way you develop any other skill or habit—*practice*! You must make a conscious effort to cultivate the art of self-discipline in your life and refuse to settle for less than your own personal best. Take a cue from any of your heroes whom you esteem. They are the ones who stayed the course and attained their dream in spite of the challenges they had to face.

All true champions have mastered the principle of discipline: the Olympic athlete who rises at 4:00 AM each morning to workout, the salesperson who makes cold calls in spite of one rejection after another in order to generate a sale, the concert pianist who plays for hours to perfect one stanza. Your desire to cultivate this principle will bring you greater success in every area of your life. Begin by realizing that you are part of the influence that determines the outcome of your destiny. Affirm with yourself, your obligation to see your dreams come true. Develop a detailed plan of action to accomplish your goals. Your ability to remain faithful to your plan will grow, despite the ever-present obstacles, as you master the principle of discipline.

- **Employ the strategies below to help you cultivate the principle of Discipline:**

  1. Deny yourself something you really enjoy for thirty days, such as, eating sweets, shopping, watching TV.

  2. Make a new commitment to complete every project you start no matter what.

3. Remind yourself, every day, your choices control your destiny.

4. Study the characteristics of high achievers you admire—adapt and adopt their methods for discipline.

FAILURE

FAILURE: THE CONDITION OR FACT OF NOT ACHIEVING THE DESIRED END.

Abraham Lincoln is one of our best-known and accomplished presidents. Yet, President Lincoln knew more about failure than most. He failed as a businessman and a farmer. He failed in his first attempt to run for the Illinois legislature. When he sought the office of speaker, he failed as well. He failed in his initial effort for the U.S. House of Representatives. He failed in his pursuit to be appointed to the United States Land Office. Twice he was unsuccessful in his race for the U.S. Senate. In 1856, he even failed in his nomination for the vice presidency. How is it that a man who became acquainted with so much disappointment in pursuit of his ambitions, could go on to become president of the United States? Lincoln was not just any president, but one of the greatest in our nation's history. Through the pain of his journey, he refused to question the authenticity of his destiny. In addition, he courageously changed the face of a nation by abolishing slavery—one of the greatest atrocities in American history. President Lincoln did not recognize failure. Instead he *insisted* failure *recognize him.*

Most people believe that if we fail at something, it somehow diminishes who we are as a person. And many of us see failure as a fatal result, a form of death, a point of no return or some type of permanent condition. Bill Copland, a business executive in the Charlotte area, once told me, "Failure is only temporary. Giving up is what makes it permanent." Many of us are so afraid of what others may think if we fail that we never try to pursue our passions. What stops us from taking action? Fear! What is fear? *Fear is an emotion of apprehension, creating false images of failure prior to the pursuit of your ambitions.* Your fears are like border patrols of your own mind enforcing self-imposed limitations. Goals and fears co-exist for good reasons. The essence of any goal is to expand your life beyond your current state or circumstances. What is the number one fear most of us have? Failure, right? It's not really failure we fear. In many cases, the perceived *by-product* of failure is actually our main concern. Our fear arises from the assumption that failure will lead to rejection from our friends and family. If we fail, they will not love us anymore. If we fail, they will judge us. If we fail, our parents, our companion, or our spouse will be hurt and embarrassed. And there is always our fear of losing our so-called prized possessions, our home, the cars we drive and other status symbols.

Yet, everybody experiences failure at one time or another. If your love ones are shamed or discontented, by you falling short in pursuit of a really difficult goal, it's because they could never see your vision. In our failures, we acquire true growth and prosperity. A baseball player who hits 300 is considered a good player. Yet he gets a hit only three out of every ten at-bats. In other words, he fails to get a hit 70 percent of the time! Statistics say most professional salespeople have a *close ratio* between 10–30 percent depending upon the product they sell. Yet, selling is reported as the highest paid profession in the world. In business entities, failure is recognized as a common occurrence. Most companies have established a *failure department* to help them learn from their mistakes. This department is known to us as the research and development department. Many of the luxuries we enjoy today were mistakenly discovered while inventors and developers were attempting to create something totally different. So, learn to view failure as a necessary stop on your journey to success. The truth is: you cannot fail if you do not *try*! In other words, if you are not failing, chances are you are not willing to explore new heights or move outside of the area you have already mastered.

IF YOU ARE NOT FAILING, CHANCES ARE YOU'RE NOT WILLING TO EXPLORE NEW HEIGHTS OR MOVE OUTSIDE THE AREA YOU HAVE ALREADY MASTERED.

Failure can be a great teacher. In sports, coaches employ a *success through failure* perspective. Every time a coach calls a *time out*, the game is interrupted to quickly correct the failures of the team's planned execution. The coach, in real time, highlights exactly where the team is failing, and instructs them in their corrective action. In practice, during the game, after the game, over and over again the athlete goes through this routine of development. During this process, the athlete learns success through failure. Sports can be defined as a developmental seminar in excellence. As an athlete, your coach guides you through a repetitious and strategic process of fundamentals and discipline, to develop flawless execution. Using this tool creates a psychological and physiological capacity to win; thereby resulting in the ability to consistently produce victories over loses! When athletes adopt this practice, they indoctrinate a champion mentality.

Scouting is another power tool coaches employ to develop athletes into champions. It is used by coaches of every sport to gain a competitive edge on the rival. During halftime and again after the game, the coach guides the team through the process of *success through failure.* By watching the film of the game, the coach and players are able to study the tendencies and failures of the opponent, their own teammates and themselves. Golfers videotape their golf swing to see their own mechanical failures for true authentic correction. Imagine what could happen if you applied this practice to review your failed experiences.

So, as we experience mistakes and failure in our everyday lives, we have to learn how to stop, take time, study, and review our actions. If you try to do something and it does not work, you must learn all you can from the experience. Solicit the advice of an expert or a knowledgeable and supportive acquaintance, regroup and move forward. When you learn how to employ these strategies in your life, your failures become stepping stones for success.

Mastering the principle of handling failure and disappointment can be the greatest of all attributes for life survival. Champions, peak performers, and high achievers use the acquired knowledge of their failed attempts to increase their odds of succeeding the next time. If you fall short, remember with each effort, you will attain a new understanding of what it takes to accomplish your goal. You have to keep trying until the odds are in your favor.

Throughout the history of mankind, civilization has progressed more through failure than success. Learn to handle failure because it will separate you from the crowd. Once your heart is set on doing something special, you will become an individual incapable of allowing setbacks to stand in your way. You will begin to view them as a minor detour on the road to your heart's desires.

THROUGHOUT THE HISTORY OF MANKIND, CIVILIZATION HAS PROGRESSED MORE THROUGH FAILURE THAN SUCCESS.

Your ability to handle failure and disappointment also plays a major role in your attitude toward life. When we put our whole heart into a project and things do not work out, we will be disappointed. It is only natural to feel some sense of frustration at the outcome. Those who pretend nothing bothers them, become a walking powder keg, and at some point they will explode. But those who walk around gloomy and despondent—*Woe is me*—are only making matters worse. It is important not to keep things bottled up, but equally important not to wallow in your misery. You must devise a strategy to quickly release feelings of helplessness, failure, and any other nonproductive emotion.

One helpful strategy is to form or join a support team of like-minded individuals who are committed to higher levels of achievement. A support team is a wonderful concept many achievers employ. Members of your support team will lend an attentive ear when you need to vent your anger. They will build you up when you are torn down. Most important, they will remind you of your talents and the importance of accomplishing your goals. Additionally, control your environment by surrounding yourself with compatible individuals, positive thinkers, and those pursuing a life of significance.

Regular exercise is used by many as a tool for stress management to help cope with life's challenges. It will assist you with staying healthy and make you less prone to illness during challenging times. Medical research has proven that your mind and body are intimately connected, and your thoughts can affect your *physical well-being*. Exercise has the remarkable capacity to help reduce the anxiety created by antagonizing thoughts and emotions which may be dominating your mind. After a good workout, you will feel revitalized and ready to tackle the problem once more.

Another great way to handle disappointment is to do something nice for someone else. It will take your mind off your own problem and give you a warm glow of satisfaction from helping someone. Please know that no good deed goes unrewarded. The values you practice in your everyday life produce karma; a divine force which reciprocates actions that eventually make its way back to you.

WHEN YOU FAIL, YOU SHOULD GAIN EXPERIENCE AND KNOWLEDGE YOU DID NOT POSSESS BEFOREHAND.

So, do not wither when you suffer temporary defeat in your life. It will happen. Acknowledge, to yourself and others who support you, how you truly feel. Do not allow your pride to prevent you from exercising this strategy. Acknowledging your failure is healthy, if you reposition yourself in a productive state of mind. Even when you fail, you should gain experience and knowledge you did not posses beforehand. This knowledge increases your ability to accomplish your goal. Be persistent in your efforts to succeed. Study the lesson in your letdowns, and you will triumph over every hurdle as you learn how to handle disappointment and failure. Allow yourself the freedom to be afraid to fail, to succeed and move forward. There is nothing wrong with failing, as long as you are failing forward!

- **Employ the strategies below to help you cultivate the principle of handling Failure:**

    1. Do not ask, "Why is this happening to me?" Begin by asking yourself, "What is happening? How is this going to change or affect my life? How do I respond?"

    2. Prepare yourself mentally to embrace the changes in your life.

    3. Take time to analyze and document what you have learned from the experience. This will assist you in a successful completion in your next attempt.

    4. Find or form a group of like-minded people who will be your sounding board, your support system, a team who will be there to get you through the tough times and remind you of your worth.

    5. Develop a *Failure Fallback Plan*. The next time you fail, have a plan for what you can do to tackle the demons of frustration and disappointment. Choose something that will restore your sense of accomplishment, a competitive exercise, playing a musical instrument, or cooking, to remind yourself that a failed attempt does not define you.

MENTAL TOUGHNESS

✦

MENTAL TOUGHNESS: EMOTIONAL
RESILIENCE OF CONVICTIONS AND OUTLOOK;
NOT
EASILY INFLUENCED OR DIVERTED BY
SENTIMENT OR IMPEDIMENTS.

Nelson Mandela exemplified mental toughness in his lifetime commitment and struggle for democracy. Mandela said it best himself, "The struggle is my life, and is not to be taken lightly." Mr. Mandela was held as a political prisoner for opposing apartheid. For nearly *three decades* he suffered and endured unlawful prison confinement without being able to see family, children, or even his wife. Despite all he sacrificed, Mandela still *twice* flatly rejected offers of immediate release on the condition he renounce his opposition to apartheid and violence. In 1993, three years after being released, Mandela accepted the Nobel Peace Prize. In addition to all his accomplishments, on May 10, 1994, he became the first democratically elected state president of South Africa. Today, he continues to fight against apartheid at the mature age of eighty-nine. Mandela remains South Africa's best-known and loved hero. Nelson Mandela personifies true mental toughness in his sacrifice, determination, and the *commitment to his convictions*.

Picture yourself for a moment, confined to a room for almost thirty years. Now imagine if all you had to do to regain your liberty, was to just stop opposing injustice. The confinement would be difficult, but adjusting your perspective to reclaim your freedom would be easy. On the success journey everyone will encounter what feels like insurmountable obstacles. While there may be many strategies one can use, in most cases, your sheer ability to hang tough will see you through most difficult situations. It is this *mental makeup* of high achievers that most people often fail to understand. It is easy to recognize athletic dexterity, intellectual capacity, a pleasing personality, and other obvious traits associated with winners. But psychological strength is not physically visible. Yet, you cannot truly succeed without the ability to manage your mind, forcing it to concentrate only on the task at hand. Without the attribute of mental toughness, your mind will cause you to shrink in a crisis, rendering you incapable of tapping the full power of your God-given ability to overcome obstacles. Those who have climbed the mountain of success have learned the power of being mentally tough.

People who succeed on a massive scale have developed the capacity to handle pressure in situations where the outcome is uncertain. It is the executive who accepts the challenge of turning around a division or company mired in groupthink and rigidity, incapable of coping with a changing world. It is the athlete who wants the ball, when the game is on the line. It is the schoolteacher who readily accepts the call to teach those students labeled *unreachable*. All who have mastered the art of mental toughness know there's a chance of failure in accepting a complicated task, yet they relish the opportunity to stretch themselves to the limit, because it is part of the essence of life. We must be willing to fail, or there can be no growth in our lives. However, the joy of conquering what most people dare not even attempt, gives the tough-minded a sense of accomplishment others will never know.

PEOPLE WHO SUCCEED ON A MASSIVE SCALE HAVE DEVELOPED THE CAPACITY TO HANDLE PRESSURE IN SITUATIONS WHERE THE OUTCOME IS UNCERTAIN.

To master the art of mental toughness, you must truly believe in your ability to succeed. There has never been a winner who did not believe he or she *deserved to win*. Expect to win more often than not and you will. As you increase your desire for success at whatever you do, your self-confidence will grow immensely. You will no longer be so easily deterred by the challenges you encounter along your journey. You will know you are becoming mentally tough when you refuse to quit, and you are able to persevere to reach one of your most challenging goals.

I invite you to catch the fever for life and become a man or woman on fire for your most deep set desires. There is no question enthusiasm motivates others. In the words of Dennis Kimbro, "set yourself on fire, and observe how many people will come to watch you burn." As people begin to see the passion you have for your pursuit, many will be drawn to you in your quest, again creating the *magnetic effect*. Decide today to become mentally tougher. Seek challenges, which will cause you to dig deep within to find the inner resources necessary for success. Once you know you have what it takes to succeed in a big way, the world will no longer seem such an overwhelming place. Instead, it becomes a venue for you to do something special with your life. By developing your mental toughness, you will experience the joy of consistently winning and achieving your outstanding goals.

- **Employ the strategies below to help you cultivate the principle of Mental Toughness:**

  1. Be absolutely clear on the purpose of your dreams and passions. Record your purpose in writing; refer to it when obstacles appear. You will be reminded of *why* you choose this pursuit. Being reminded of *why*, will reinforce your drive to go over, under, around, or through your obstacles, never allowing them to stop you.

  2. Establish clearly defined goals and intentions, and outline the steps required to achieve them so you will always have a roadmap to fall back on if you get *LOST* along the way.

  3. Make an agreement with yourself. No matter how long it takes in the pursuit of what you want, never abandon your dreams. Every time you feel defeated or feel like giving up, force yourself to take *one more step*. A mantra is also useful in cultivating mental strength, such as, "I am a trailblazer and I blaze the trail for others." Repeat it to yourself over and over.

  4. Make an agreement with yourself to remain dedicated to your values and beliefs, even when faced with Goliath opposition. Always remember, when the going gets tough, the tough get going.

LEADERSHIP

✦

LEADERSHIP: THE ABILITY TO GUIDE OR SHOW THE WAY; A MEANS OF BRINGING SOMETHING TO A PARTICULAR CONDITION OR RESULT.

During the 1980 NBA Championship Finals, Hall of Fame and six-time NBA champion, Kareem Abdul Jabbar, became injured and unable to play for the remainder of the finals. Kareem was the Lakers' number one offensive and defensive weapon. Losing Kareem hit the Lakers hard. The confidence of the players, the coaches, and the fans was definitely rattled. While the players were wondering what to do and how they would possibly win without Kareem, Ervin 'Magic' Johnson, then in his first season of the NBA, stood up in the middle of the team huddle, looked his coach Pat Riley in the face, and told, him "I am going to play the center position in place of Kareem." Magic made the decision to switch from the point guard position to the center position. Never in the history of the NBA had there been a player who was interchangeable from the point guard to the center position, this was unheard of since the point guard is typically the shortest player and the center is the tallest. Magic Johnson, as a rookie, played all five positions, was named MVP, and led his team in capturing the 1980 NBA Championship. Magic's courageous decision was the heart of a champion and a leader, which was the birth of his legacy. The Los Angles Lakers won five NBA Championships under the leadership of Magic Johnson. In Magic's legacy, he is known as an encourager, with the ability to make others better.

THE NATURE OF A PERSON'S SPIRIT SPEAKS TO THE NATURE HE OR SHE MANIFESTS.

Leadership encompasses all of the principles discussed in this book: purpose, responsibility, self-control, consistency, discipline, handling failure and disappointment, mental toughness, and inner peace. We all have leadership ability. However, for most of us, it resides dormant within, but for many others it is actively present. Sometimes it is conscious and at other times it is unconscious. No matter what your status, leadership will automatically activate itself when circumstances require it. Case in point: when Kareem was injured during the NBA Finals, Magic's natural leadership was activated. Leadership may be stimulated by any number of conditions. In this chapter, I will discuss with you four types of leadership, each stirred by certain major circumstances.

- Natural

- Humanitarian

- Purposeful

- Spontaneous

Natural Leadership is inherent. It is activated by well-meaning intentions to organize and oversee different projects. We are all familiar with these individuals; he or she chaired the event committee for the high school prom. If they were part of the faculty, he or she presided over every event on and off campus. These individuals also volunteered to coach the church basketball team. They even planned the church picnic. Many of us were lucky enough to have them as our boss. As our boss, they left a lasting impression on our lives. They also carry a high level of self-confidence in their ability to create a teachable, but fun-loving environment. All who know them would never forget them, because they had fun, felt loved, grew personally and learned life lessons under their leadership. These individuals' actions were motivated by their natural desire to help and see others do well.

Humanitarian Leadership is held by those with the gift of compassion and may be activated during a time when aid or assistance is needed by others. These individuals, once made aware of a human need, cannot ignore the pain or suffering of others. They have to heed their calling. Clara Hale, "Mother Hale," of Hale House, who was discussed in the first chapter, exemplified leadership of humanity in her innate desire to give unwanted children the love and support they so desperately needed. Since leaving the White House, former president Jimmy Carter, has used his status to negotiate peace and to fight diseases. The Carter Center was established in 1992 with the mandate of resolving political conflict and combating disease. In 2001, the Guinea Worm Disease became a disease of the world's forgotten people, the poorest of the poor, in thirteen African countries including Sudan, Ghana, and Nigeria. The Carter Center was recognized for its health effort, for near-total eradication of the disease. In 2002, Carter was awarded the Nobel Peace Prize for his decades of untiring efforts to find solutions to international conflicts, to advance democracy and human rights, and to promote economic and social development.

Purposeful Leadership is initiated by one's inborn desire for basic survival and human rights. In many cases, Purposeful Leadership is activated by someone being required to take the lead position in a necessary cause. Nelson Mandela and Dr. Martin Luther King Jr. demonstrated Purposeful Leadership. Mandela is well-known for his lifetime commitment against apartheid and the struggle for democracy. Dr. King, Mandela, John F. Kennedy, and many others felt called by a life mission. Mandela was imprisoned for nearly thirty years, because of his battle to rid South Africa of apartheid and violence. Both, Dr. King as the drum major for justice and Mandela as the commander-in-chief for democracy, lead movements that changed the government laws and policies of an entire country. Dr. King was assassinated for his fight to obtain basic human rights and equal justice for himself and other minorities. Those who exemplify *Purposeful Leadership* have a calling. They are willing to die for the great causes they champion. Dr. King was awarded the Nobel Peace Prize in 1964 for his fight to obtain racial equality and his commitment to nonviolence and Mandela was awarded a Nobel Peace Prize and the presidency of his country.

Spontaneous Leadership is activated by emergency circumstances. These individuals are thrust into a situation, which requires immediate action on their part. At home or work they are unassuming people. But in an emergency, their inner character of consideration for people and human life is prompted. For instance, let's say your church catches fire in the middle of worship service. A Spontaneous Leader, without any conscious thought will risk his or her own life, *leading* people to safety, while most are running away to safety. Or, maybe a group of travelers are involved in an awful bus accident. This individual may be traveling along the same route and witnesses the same accident, with others traveling the highway, but this individual is innately compelled to react, while others just curiously stand by. To the victim, the person will seem to appear from out of nowhere and begin organizing a rescue operation. They will delegate others to get people to safety, while they check on the injured and make sure no one is trapped inside the wreckage. Yet, if you ask them, how they knew what to do, they may only remember sketchy details, because their actions were stimulated unconsciously by an inherent, but spontaneous consideration for others.

As humans, we are essentially spiritual beings, going through a human experience. The nature of a person's spirit dictates the character he or she manifests. True leaders have what Dr. Myles Munroe describes as a *Spirit of Leadership*. This is a unique mental essence derived from an internalized discovery of self, which creates a strong, positive, and confident self-image, an image of self-significance. From this attitude, arises a value system of service, consideration, and compassion for others. True leaders have a sincere desire to help others achieve with the same mind-set as they. True leaders are steadfast in their integrity toward those who faithfully trust and follow their direction.

LEADERS KNOW IT'S BETTER TO DO THE RIGHT THING
THAN TO DO THINGS RIGHT.

Decision Making is also an integral part of being a leader. Leaders possess the ability to think creatively and flexibly. They recognize the solutions required and take action. Leaders do not suffer from *analysis paralysis*. They are decisive, knowing not everything will go according to plan, but confident they can make the necessary adjustments to keep moving forward. They are mindful, but not worried, when implementing solutions. They are not afraid to look within themselves for answers. Effective leaders know conditions are unlikely to be perfect for every endeavor, but they know it is better to *do the right thing,* than to *do things right.*

In a business environment, it is important to remember, policies and procedures are in place to provide consistent methods for handling common occurrences. However, understand no set of rules applies to every situation. For example, I will share my unfortunate experience while employed by a major company in Charlotte, North Carolina. One of my beloved uncles died, and as any normal, caring relative, I requested voluntary time off without pay (VTO) from work to attend his funeral. But the company policy (*Doing Things Right*) only allows three days of bereavement for immediate family (parents, siblings, spouse, or children). Since he was not considered *immediate family*, as narrowly defined, my request was denied. The rationale was based on understaffing and the resolution offered by my operations manager, instead was to call in sick; a statement lacking integrity. Life isn't as *black* and *white* as a company policy. Many of us are raised by individuals other than our biological parents, and many of us have brothers and sisters who were not acquired by birth, but by special human connection.

Death should *always* be an excusable request, certainly worth consideration beyond the established rules as there is only one opportunity to *pay your last respects* to a loved one. Good leadership has empathy for others. In my case, management showed neither empathy nor sympathy. Good leadership would (*Doing the Right Thing*) have granted a VTO. If you are the decision maker in this type of situation—policy versus people—a good guide would be to treat others as you would want to be treated under the same circumstances. An employee may not jump for joy by your decision to approve a VTO because it would probably fall under human expectation. On the other hand, they will not forget how devalued you made them feel as a staff member. There is no way to measure the damage to employee morale created by insensitive decisions. In the end, I was unable to attend my uncles' funeral.

Leadership requires the capacity to rally yourself and others around a worthwhile cause. For example, you may know of a tragic accident caused by a drunk driver which leaves two infants without their parents, and you are moved to help. Many laws are initiated at the community level, by one person with leadership, inspired to make a difference. You do not have to be the president, chief, or the head of a group to be a leader, nor is every head in an organization equipped to lead. If one has been placed in a high status of an organization, the *position* does not *magically create* leadership within that person. The only thing for certain is someone has been given great responsibility. Responsibility requires great virtue. The qualities that distinguish an effective leader are; flexibility, decisiveness, fortitude, serviceability, and the ability to recognize and cultivate the leader in others.

In a corporate or professional setting, part of that responsibility is accepting fault when your staff or team fails. In today's environment, if a person or a team falls short of the expected result in his or her job or position, the interpretation is the *staff* failed. A true leader understands he or she actually failed in managing, coaching, developing, encouraging, or mentoring the selected individual or individuals. As observed by the disciple Timothy, "A bishop then must be blameless, the husband of one wife, vigilant, sober, of good behavior, given to hospitality, apt to teach; not given to wine, no striker, not greedy of filthy lucre; but patient, not a brawler, not covetous …" (1Timothy 3:2–3 KJV).

Leadership has become a role one plays rather than a life one leads. Real leadership is not just a label, but is manifested in developing and guiding the performance and results of others. True leaders do not seek power but are driven by a passion to achieve a noble cause. Leaders often stand alone in unpopular or risky circumstances. All the money in the world can make you affluent and having great influence can make you powerful, but wealth and power can never make you a leader.

LEADERSHIP HAS BECOME A ROLE ONE PLAYS, RATHER THAN A LIFE ONE LEADS.

Everyone has latent leadership skills, and these skills can be used in a variety of settings—work, social groups, and professional organizations. In fact, leading and influencing a group of *volunteers* is an ideal way to hone your leadership skills. I'm talking about a team or group of individuals who will commit to results without the motivation of money or the fear of career consequences. To lead a volunteer group, you need to effectively communicate with your team members. Show them the vision of the project to obtain their buy-in of the venture. Be a person of integrity and foster good relations with others. Former United State Senator, Alan Kooi Simpson said it best, "If you have integrity nothing else matters. If you don't have integrity nothing else matters." Others will eagerly listen to you if you have earned their respect. Every person on a team desires to be successful. If they have confidence in you, they will be motivated to follow your lead and make the mission a success.

Real leaders are people of great vision. They see things not as they are but in the possibility of what they could be. "Where there is no vision the people will perish" (Proverbs 29:18 KJV). I suggest life offers no right or wrong way of doing things. Instead, there are just different methods to accomplish a task. However, some methods will certainly be more effective than others. You may not always be familiar with the most effective strategies, but you will discover them if you are open to new ideas and willing to take risks. Tap into the part of you, which can look beyond the present and give you a vision for the future. Be progressive in your outlook, knowing nothing stays the same. The only constant in this world is change. Become a change agent by becoming a visionary. Constantly look for opportunities to contribute, by helping to make people and things better. Seize the chance to lead efforts to bring about positive change. Most problems can be solved with the help of well-meaning individuals willing to take a position of leadership.

To develop your leadership skills, look for opportunities to challenge yourself by chairing a community or church project. Your leadership skills will increase as you take on new ventures. Tap into your leadership potential. You will find great rewards when you begin to assert yourself as a leader.

- **Employ the strategies below to help you cultivate the principle of Leadership:**

    1. Invest money and time for leadership development—read books, listen to audio speeches, and attend seminars.

    2. Volunteer to chair a committee or project at your church or a business or civic organization.

    3. Look for opportunities in your work to take on leadership assignments—take on a project, volunteer for an unpopular task.

    4. Exhibit leadership qualities in whatever you do—this will increase your likelihood of being placed in a leadership position, whether it is a promotion at work, a new job, or as the officer of an organization.

INNER PEACE

✦

*INNER PEACE: A STATE OF BEING FREE OF
CONTENTION PSYCHOLOGICALLY AND
SPIRITUALLY; AN ARRIVAL AT TRANQUILITY,
SELF-ACCEPTANCE, CONTENTMENT
AND BALANCE IN SPIRIT, MIND, AND BODY.*

Everyone desires to experience inner peace—a sense of tranquility, balance in spirit, mind, body and heart. True inner peace can be found deeply rooted in our faith and belief in a Supreme Source, the Grandmaster of the universe. This Source is referred to by many names. You may have heard these names among the list: God, Yahweh, Allah, Jehovah, Emmanuel, Creator, and Father. The name is not important, but it is paramount you respect and *trust* the Source. Faith is defined as a secure belief in God and a trusting acceptance of God's will. In the rat race of everyday living, obtaining an inner peace can be extremely difficult. But it can be done if you find time for yourself. It is essential to slow down long enough to be alone with yourself. It is extremely important to take time to do *nothing*. Make it a priority to schedule time each day for yourself, to relax alone for meditation. During your quiet time, get acquainted with the internal you, the genius within, the God within you, the Grand Source. Invest your time in uncovering what is important to you and mapping the path to achieve your objectives. Calm your nerves and remain as still as possible. Think deeply about the things that concern you. Allow the Grand Source of your existence to speak to you and listen intently. Breathe deeply and feel yourself operating on a higher plane.

TRUE INNER PEACE CAN ONLY BE FOUND AT THE ROOT OF OUR FAITH.

You will not possess inner peace until you choose a path that your heart delights. "Delight thyself also in the LORD: and he shall give thee the desires of thine heart" (Psalms 37:4 KJV) When you are at peace, you are in touch with the inner person, and your activities are guided by a value system which promotes well-being and the need to achieve. When you are at peace with yourself, you will radiate self-confidence. When you have a sense of inner peace, your relationships with others will improve dramatically. As you encounter people in your everyday walk, they will respond to the inner person you are projecting. Are you insecure and unsure of yourself, or are you confident, focused, and happy to be experiencing this miracle called life? Your thinking and attitude will show in what you say and do, and others will react to you accordingly.

AS YOU ENCOUNTER PEOPLE IN YOUR EVERYDAY WALK,
THEY ARE RESPONDING TO THE INNER PERSON YOU ARE PROJECTING.

One of the quickest ways to develop the inner confidence you want to radiate is to accomplish something. Decide to do something you have thought about doing, but somehow put on the back burner. Run a 5K race, audition for a community play, build a deck, or paint a portrait—anything. Just get started, and finish it. Accomplishing anything outside of your normal routine will be a powerful stimulator. Pretty soon, you will want to do more. Give of yourself in service to others, whether you are recognized for your efforts or not. Even if no one else says, "thank you," thank yourself and smile.

GIVE OF YOURSELF IN SERVICE TO OTHERS, WHETHER
YOU ARE RECOGNIZED FOR YOUR EFFORTS OR NOT.

Life is quite challenging at times. However, your job is to live life to the fullest, growing in wisdom each day. By learning from your own mistakes, as well as the mistakes of others, you can celebrate your victories and enjoy your contact with others. Make it a point to be open and honest with yourself. Admit at times, you are clueless. In the past, it was difficult for me to admit when I felt intellectually challenged in my ability to successfully head certain projects. In order to attain true inner peace within our own and others' imperfections, we must love one another *unconditionally.* "Thou shalt not avenge, nor bear any grudge against the children of thy people, but thou shalt love thy neighbour as thyself: I am the LORD" (Leviticus 19:18 KJV). We must believe in the Source as the determining higher power, and hold the Source in reverence. You need to know that this Source has dominion over all the cosmos, which works with us and for us.

The karma we produce in our everyday lives should reflect this Source. The *Good Book* admonishes us on the golden rule in Matthew 7:12, "Therefore all things whatsoever ye would that men should do to you, do ye even so to them: for this is the law and the prophets." (KJV) *Do unto others as you would have them to do unto you.* If you work hard in pursuit of your passions and treat people fair and just, positive things will definitely happen for you. But know this; in spite of all your good works, you will experience heartbreaking moments in your life. So, resolve to respect and trust the Grand Source. As you master the art of living a balanced life of honesty and tolerance, even in the most distressing times, you will posses true inner peace. "The God of my rock; in him I will trust ..." (2 Samuel 22:3 KJV).

- **Employ the strategies below to help you cultivate the principle of Inner Peace:**

    1. Set aside fifteen minutes every day for prayer or meditation. Force yourself to clear your mind and be still—listen to the still, small voice within.

    2. Take on some kind of volunteer work, doing something worthwhile for others. It will give you a sense of satisfaction and well-being.

3. Just as you crave appreciation for what you do, be sure to show appreciation to others and what they do.

4. Make these four agreements with yourself:

   • I agree to always be true to myself, even if it makes me uncomfortable initially.

   • I agree to disagree with others and move forward, without taking it personally.

   • I agree it is OK to be wrong and to laugh at myself.

   • I agree to accept and work on the things I can control, while acknowledging and letting go of those out of my control.

5. Take time to accomplish something outside of your normal routine—(Run a 5K race; audition for a community play; build a deck for your home; learn to swim; or play the piano).

My Dream

My personal life story began in a small southern nook in the world. Mobile, Alabama, is a port city in the Deep South, affectionately nick named LA (Lower Alabama) by the legendary recording artist James Brown, often referred to as the "Godfather of Soul." In my hometown there is a church on every corner. My childhood was rich in God, love, and family fellowship from my close-knit Christian family. Even my teenage years were filled with joy and pride. I grew up in a family of extremely talented gospel singers and musicians. We were community celebrities if you will.

Even as a young boy surrounded by all the flattery and family cama-raderie, I knew I had a destiny beyond Thursday night rehearsals and singing all day on Sunday with my siblings and relatives. However, like many of you, I tried to honor my parents' attempt to manage and assist me in the direction of a so-called *secure career*. My parents told me, "Work hard, go to college, and find a good job." I know what you're thinking. We must have the same parents. No, not the same parents, however, our parents may have used the same success model. Success has a unique meaning for each individual. No two people will have the same definition of success. Success can be defined first as dreaming, then doing the things necessary to put yourself in the position to work in your dream career. Success is not just a *good job*, in fact, *good* is rela-tive, and a *job* is employment provided by the success of someone else's *dream*.

In today's work environment of downsizing and right sizing, jobs come and go. Here in Charlotte, I have been witness to many banking professionals going back and forth between Wachovia Bank and Bank of America in an effort to maintain employment after being victim to staff reduction initiatives. We fail to realize that during these very times, we should take the opportunity to pause, reflect and reconsider our vocational and personal path!

Like many of you, I had to discover that being uncertain about my direction was part of the journey to my true destiny. Even as I took my final exam while in my first year of college, I knew my education was at odds with my true fate. I had no idea what my dream career resembled, but I knew it wasn't Electrical Engineering Technology. I asked myself two questions to gain some understanding in my life. What is my purpose for being here in school? Why did I choose this curriculum? I knew I could earn a *good* income in the technology field. And I knew it would please my parents, but I just couldn't leverage enough enthusiasm based on *The Whys*, the reasons to complete the curriculum. I needed more, I dreamed of something bigger. Deep within, I could feel my purpose was something larger. After taking my final exam, there were three questions I asked myself: "Can this be all there is to life?" "How long will I desire to work in this field?" "What would I really like to do with my life?" This was a difficult point of confusion and mixed emotions. I had been unable to rid myself of the feeling that I was just going through the motions, and then I met Reginald "Reggie" Brown.

TO PLEASE MY PARENTS AND TO MAKE A LIVING.

It is not clear to me how we initially met, but we were kindred spirits. We would talk for hours about life, our dreams, and our ambitions. The more we talked the more I felt I wanted to be like this guy! Reginald had many admirable qualities. He was handsome, well-dressed, confident, articulate, and he had a great smile. He was an accomplished baseball athlete and graduate of Florida A & M University. He had been the roommate of Hall of Fame baseball player, Vince Coleman. But when I met Reggie, he was a disgusted professional with National Cash Register, Inc. (NCR). He shared with me his discontentment with his life. Reggie was certain his future entailed something much larger than his current achievements. I got the feeling he was very unhappy. He was clearly intelligent and one of the most competitively driven people I had ever met. Reggie, with all he had going for himself—a college degree, hardworking with the "good job"—was miserable because he had no *personal* fulfillment. Being fulfilled and satisfied with your life, knowing each day is an opportune gift for the taking, is paramount for the journey and is also the greatest part of your destiny. As you can imagine, this caused me to ponder my situation even more. I thought very seriously and honestly about my *whys* for being in the engineering program—*to please my parents* and *to make a living*. I remember thinking, "This could be me in five years."

Four weeks later, I withdrew from college. Reggie, his friend Paul, and I partnered to form a new business. We opened an auto detailing company. At last I had found it, not my purpose, but a feeling of purpose. I had discovered a motivation I never felt before. I was excited and bursting with enthusiasm about the possibilities of the new company. I then thought of an idea to get back the money I had spent for tuition. I ran a special promotion for the school faculty. I met with Mr. Smyth, the school president to discuss my idea and to my surprise, he became my first customer. This was a pivotal moment in my life. There I was, twenty years old, now driven with a purpose, with the ability to walk into my college presidents' private office, conduct a feature and benefit presentation of our new company, and walk out with the keys to his sports car, without being insured or bonded!

Both Mr. Smyth and I were completely unaware of the significance of his decision. This experience taught me, in many cases, *we have not, because we ask not*. This confirmed: if you prepare, launch out, take action, display a good image, demonstrate confidence, and exhibit character and competence, you can accomplish uncommon success in common hours. *<Preparation + Action + Appearance + Attitude + Professionalism = Positive Results>*. When I left Mr. Smyth's office my confidence level was extremely high, I felt invincible. So I headed over to Crown Mercedes, the number one Mercedes dealer in Birmingham, Alabama. When I returned to our shop with a 420 SEL Mercedes Benz, Reggie looked at me and yelled at the top of his voice, "Who in the hell's car is that!?" In an unassuming, but confident voice, I responded, "It belongs to Crown Mercedes." He was angry, with concern about the financial liability if something had happened, because we were still uninsured. We stood in silence and stared at one another for what seemed like thirty minutes, and then he just exploded in laughter. Reggie accepted and acknowledged my gift of persuasion. He welcomed the unexpected revenue as well. We secured contracts with several major companies. We became an unstoppable sales duo. Another defining moment was securing a contract with the Winfrey Hotel. The hotel was built in collaboration with the Galleria Mall, a coming attraction to the city of Birmingham. We really got off to a good start, but lacking patience and the discipline for delayed gratification, the partners gave up before reaching the goal.

LACKING PATIENCE AND DISCIPLINE FOR DELAYED GRATIFICATION, THE PARTNERS GAVE UP BEFORE REACHING THE GOAL.

Personally, I was done with the traditional school-to-work model. Free enterprise had a calling on my life, like a minister to the gospel! I packed my bags and headed for Atlanta. Later, I duplicated the business model with a couple of newfound partners. In this endeavor, it was not the lack of patience or discipline to endure a long-term goal, but rather greed as the primary cause of our collapse.

After a second failed Carwash venture, I was desperate and looking for work. My brother Prentice, aware of my situation, arranged an interview with IBM. Sticking to what I learned during my experience with Mr. Smyth, I applied the principles of preparation, action, appearance, attitude, and professionalism. As a result, IBM hired me without a college degree. I was off to Charlotte and excited about the idea of a regular salary with a Fortune 500 company. One of my proudest accomplishments while at IBM was ironically, through a false-hearted opportunity.

I had been assigned to evaluate and conduct a report on the Suggestion Program. The Suggestion Program was designed to promote employee creativity and an "inventor environment." IBM would pay an employee up to $150,000.00 for a process improvement idea. But the staff had become disillusion with the program bureaucracy. I was one of the employees that had just filed a complaint about the programs' process. My immediate management decided they were going to teach me a lesson. However, as life would have it, senior management was so impressed with my report that I was asked to present my report at our All Hands meetings.

The All Hands meeting was a forum for the general manager to review the company's annual goals. Typically the general manager was the sole presenter. To think, I was asked to present my findings to over 5000 co-workers, among them the best and brightest minds in America—scholars from Purdue, Vanderbilt, and MIT. This was a huge opportunity for me to demonstrate my oral talents. What's the moral of the story? When God blesses you with a talent, it doesn't matter who is among you. We are all meant to make an impact on the world. My contribution turned out to be for the greater good personally and for the company. But again, the original intent of my speaking opportunity was not from a genuine place among management.

After seven years of feeling like a wasted resource and being extremely underutilized, I left during the company's first ever staff reduction. My morale and self-esteem was at an all-time low. I was depressed and extremely unhappy. Dejavu, I thought to myself, I'm Reggie Brown.

I felt restricted, unappreciated, and unaccomplished. *What's worse than being used; being wasted?* I needed a feeling of purpose in my life. I was only working to maintain the conventional, pre-sculpted, lifestyle of *making a living to pay bills.* My aim should have been to reach a place where I could dictate to life and choose my path based on personal enjoyment. Instead, I followed the path I was trained to follow; trying to live the *alleged American Dream,* instead of living my own dream! I needed to follow what was inside of me and I needed to be tested. I maintained an unsettled desire to run my own company. Following this feeling, I decided to explore the world of free enterprise once again. I truly believe one should *live their making* instead of *making a living.* In other words, strive to achieve your full potential using your gifts and talents rather than focusing on the superficial. The reward is much greater.

I WAS TRYING TO LIVE THE WORLD'S VERSION OF THE AMERICAN DREAM, INSTEAD OF LIVING MY OWN DREAM.

In September of 1994, I asked my functional manager at IBM to find a staff reduction package under which I could resign. Though he did find a package, he informed me I had to stay until January to receive our variable pay bonus. Not long after, in January 1995, I started ToDay Courier Service. As a young entrepreneur in the transportation industry, it certainly was difficult not having anyone to consult in my immediate family with business ownership experience. My father's brother, Uncle Henry, was a successful pastor and entrepreneur, but unfortunately he died twenty years prior to my endeavor. He is responsible for the entrepreneurial spirit that runs passionately through my veins. Uncle Greg, my mother's younger brother, is Uncle Henry's protégé. I deeply admired Uncle Greg, but I felt he was preoccupied experiencing financial challenges of his own learning curve.

Aware of the fact Uncle Greg was unfamiliar with the transportation industry, along with our twenty-year generation gap; I considered he may not be able to encourage my vision or business model. In hindsight, I was terribly mistaken in my assumption. I now realize my uncle was already serving as a mentor in my life, and was another source of guidance. However, at that point in my life, I was at a full level of being fed up. I was tired, but more importantly; I was fed up with my life situation. I just could not handle another skeptic. The only thing I felt I had left was my trust in God. With God as my guide and passion as my vehicle, I took action. I went into the unknown, excited and fueled by the possibilities of the world of free enterprise.

Whether you are pursuing a common goal or stepping into the unfamiliar, learn to enlist the help of a mentor. Mentors can be a great resource of direction in our journey through this life. What is a mentor? A mentor is someone that has been inspired with a personal desire to help you avoid some of life's danger zones or hazardous areas. Mentors invest in you for *your* own return by sharing their failures and acquired knowledge of strategies and success principles. One does not always have the availability of a mentor to ask for advice, however, when a mentor deems it necessary to give you advice, follow it. Your best friend loves you for who you are, but your mentor will not leave you the way you are. Your goals will choose your mentors. As you cruise through your day, take a moment to reflect on the people you have admired. I would guess their lives have not been perfect, yet, they have passed along valuable pearls of wisdom that can enrich your life.

In all likelihood, you may have more than one mentor. No one person is all-knowing. Different mentors will influence your life in different areas. Rev. Dr. Clifford Jones, as my pastor for over fifteen years, became my spiritual mentor, developing and shaping my growth in Christ. Joseph Greene has been one of my business mentors for over ten years, exemplifying the skills and mind-set of an entrepreneur. James Tolliver has been a personal mentor, demonstrating how to remain grounded while being an accomplished achiever. While having a mentor is advantageous for *us*, we have a social responsibility to reciprocate our experiences and life lessons for the benefit of others. We must become mentors, making a difference in the lives of others by taking an active role in helping people live their dreams. Our biggest adversary in life can be ignorance and a mind-set closed to new information or the help of others. Hence, the effectiveness of a mentor hinges on our willingness to be coached.

As president of my own company, I recognized rather quickly a few shortfalls in my business experience. I had to decide between self-employment and business ownership. Building a company was going to require tremendous growth and development on my part. I knew my strengths were in professionalism, persuasion, customer service, relationship-building, and the ability to hire good people. I was confident, if I practiced the highest level of customer service and professionalism, I would be successful. Yet, as a young business owner, I was clueless about the things I did not know. Similarly, many of you may *know what you know, but you don't know what you don't know.* As I humbled myself, I noticed there were many successful business owners that began to reach out to lend themselves as mentors. Some of my mentors would simply share advice from their pitfalls and others would instruct me on the importance of investing in myself through educational tools and seminars. A few of them invited me along and even paid my admission. I had no idea where some of them came from or why, but God had placed them in my life as interim and lifetime mentors. This phenomenon is known as the *Magnetic Affect,* whereby help comes to those who help themselves.

After nine and a half years of operation, I had to sell my company for a number of reasons: the national economic downturn following the 9/11 attacks, mistakes from my own inexperience, and being undercapitalized (*broke*). Nonetheless, I discovered neither success nor failure defines you. Rather it is your mental outlook that matters. I am proud of who I was then and who I am today, and my belief in self will define who I am tomorrow.

I believe everyone has an explicit purpose in life. Everyone's purpose can be found hidden within his or her passion. Inside your passion, you will find your motivation. Hibernating within your motivation will be the authentic you; your distinction. Each of us has a talent so individually specific that only five percent or less of the population can perform at the same level of excellence.

Like everyone else, I had dreams, and unknowingly shared those dreams with *dream killers*. Most of my dreams were created by watching what other people were saying and doing with their lives. I had desire, but I was unfamiliar with the tools and strategies necessary to take *my* dreams from conception to reality. Unconsciously, I was suffering with a low level of *self-efficacy* and with *self-limiting beliefs*. As a result, I was copying and modeling the society in which I lived, without considering, what was important to *me*. I needed to change my value system and model of success and rethink the notion of being educated and trained in a certain career to pursue the alleged *American Dream*. I asked myself, and now I am asking you, "Does the accumulation of material rewards and achievement symbols equate to true happiness?"

To answer this question, it may be useful to know human behavior is guided by a set of concrete beliefs, values, and subsequent behaviors. *<Beliefs = Values = Behaviors>* Our belief system is shaped, primarily, by family, culture, and the environment. Our behavior is merely an expression of our beliefs. The result of adopting a new belief is adapting to a new behavior pattern. For example, you may believe it is dangerous to drive without a seat belt. You probably learned this from viewing infomercials or reading a driver's manual. In the process of acquiring this new knowledge, you place a certain value on what you believe. You value your life, and therefore, wearing your seat belt becomes an important belief and behavior to you. A collective belief is a *paradigm*. It would follow that societal beliefs and values promote societal behavior.

One of the greatest paradigms of our society is about *living the American Dream.*

Our society has set a standard which suggests financial and material gain determines success. What has followed is a behavioral model in which the traditional mode is high school, college, and corporate or professional America. An older woman in my community once told me, "Don't confuse money with success." I dream of a society of individuals that value and believe in living a passion-directed life rather than conforming to traditional beliefs. I dream of an environment where people use their passion to clarify their direction and where individuals gain enough courage early in life to follow a passion-directed life. In my fifth-grade science class I became familiar with stimulus and response. I learned between a stimulus and response there is a space. In that space is our freedom and power to *choose* our response. In our response we find our growth and happiness. Humans have a choice in how to act. We get to choose what *we do, will be,* or *will become.*

In my search to find myself and my true passion in life and after years of working for other people I realized I produce my best results working for myself and on what deeply interests me. How did I go about determining my true destiny? I focused on self, I took inventory of what gave me joy and I looked at my talents and discovered the answer lived within me.

While coaching in the Charlotte NBA Pro-Am Summer Basketball League it became apparent I possessed a unique gift and found tremendous enjoyment cultivating self-efficacy and bringing out the best in people. It gave me great fulfillment to assist them in the transformation of their perspective and watching the "aha" take place in their lives. It is rewarding to see people evolve from self-limiting images, of self-doubt and mediocre thinking, to a pattern in which they thrive confidently in their chosen direction.

To become more adept at helping and empowering others, I equipped myself with tools and strategies to develop myself intellectually. I attended seminars, workshops, and lectures, took motivational psychology classes and read many empowerment books. I prayed for clear direction. As my personal knowledge expanded, I found motivation and support to pursue my dreams. I asked myself one question, "How can I help others move beyond their present condition to a more authentic action plan for living?" I envisioned The Williams Group, and in that vision is my dream and part of my life's purpose!

Today I am rewarded a career I love, and a flexible schedule with multiple streams of income. I am respected and appreciated for the impact my work has made upon others. Every week I receive a call or an e-mail from someone thanking me for an encouraging word or an insightful principle I may have shared with them. The fundamental keys to my success have been *open-mindedness,* and a *willingness* to *change.* Now, I ask you, what's *really holding you back*, what are the psychological phantoms standing between where you are and where you want to be in life?

Conclusion

How Do I Reach My True Destiny is a philosophy for living from the heart. Understand that self-knowledge grows as you subject yourself to self-examination, listen to your own thoughts, and look at your own actions. These are the principles to improve your effectiveness.

The journey of life can be like a game of basketball. Every move has significance. Accordingly, every choice we make in our lives counts. You are often your own greatest adversary, prone to self-destruction, self-sabotage, and other imaginative behaviors which move you away from your goals. Just as basketball has its rules, so does life. Now, knowing the game rules do not guarantee you will win the game every time, but disregarding the rules makes the game difficult and winning absolutely impossible.

This work is a call to *personal awareness*. It offers a fresh, honest perspective on living and an ongoing investigation of truth; the truth, about who you really are. The examined life is the one worth living. Spend your days learning how to live *your own* life. Living your own life and living it in an exceptional manner is a performing art, which requires you to do the hard work.

Every choice must serve the purpose to move you closer to your goals. As your birthright, you were given your greatest power, your power to choose. Each moment offers you a choice. It is your responsibility to exercise this power by setting and holding a direction; not being distracted and veering off course. Every decision matters. There are no insignificant choices. Even the smallest gesture has consequences. Each decision you make is either leading you toward or away from your goals. Your thoughts and your corresponding choices are the root cause of your present position. Change your thoughts and you change your life.

We know and understand destiny to be a journey of preordination. However, the choices we make from day to day custom-design and solidify our destiny. Our choices are formed by two main elements: the information we possess (knowledge) and our attitudes. Our greatest source of information is our environment. This brings to the fore the importance of expanding our environment to increase our knowledge base. We must open our minds and dedicate ourselves to an exposure of new and diverse information through a commitment of continual learning.

Attitude is the most prevailing of the two elements influencing our choices. There is nothing more powerful than attitude! Attitude shapes our world and designs our destiny. Attitude is the mind-set or psycho-logical conditioning which establishes our interpretation of, and response to, our environment. It is the manifestation of who we think we are. Religious author and authority on historical Jesus, Paul Meier said it best, "Attitudes are nothing more than habits of thought, and habits can be acquired."

The attitude of *purpose* is the first principle to discovering your true destiny. Your true destiny is hidden within your purpose, and your *passion* is the key to fulfilling your purpose. The spirit of passion is an indispensable component and serves as the engine, which drives and sustains you on your pathway to your true desires. When you are clear about what you really love to do, both your clarity and passion, guide you in creating a life of purpose. Those individuals, who exemplify a sense of discovered destiny in their level of achievement, did not do so haphazardly. They felt a purpose and possessed passion for their chosen direction. Most of us just go to work. We work our required eight hours and go home. In most cases the work we do does not drive us with a big picture of our purpose. It is simply a role we play to make money. You will know you are on the true path of your destiny, if what you do, or would like to do, has the spirit of a life assignment.

Define your purpose with a *purpose statement* and *visualize* the results you want to achieve. Set *goals* to help you realize your purpose. Take *responsibility* for your actions, knowing, no one has control over your outcomes except you. Exercise *self-control* in your pursuits, realizing, your thoughts have the greatest influence on what you do and become. Be *consistent* with your plan of action, understanding, a one-time shot at anything will not provide lasting results. Exercise *discipline* in your plan for success, not allowing outside forces to sidetrack or discourage you. Recognize *failure* is necessary in the journey of life, because it can be a great teacher. Develop *mental toughness,* to strengthen your psychological perseverance against letdowns, criticisms, and extreme adversity. Practice *leadership* in every situation so others will come to recognize your strengths and abilities. Cultivate and find *inner peace,* because true contentment and fulfillment is not possible without it.

Finally, lasting change can occur only when it takes place in the spirit of the mind. A renewed attitude is paramount to a transformed life. When a person decides to lose weight, it is a much bigger picture than just losing weight. For sustained results, there has to be a lifestyle change. It requires a changed *mental outlook* toward living a healthier lifestyle suited for the change; which includes the food you eat and regular exercise for better physical fitness. The nine principles on their own cannot change your life, but you can change your life if you are dedicated to applying them. Think about it—the principles and practices you currently use in your everyday life were learned over an entire lifetime. So, changing any perspective or behavior will require a new point of view and a repetitious application of different principles and practices.

The first step in the achievement of improved results is committing to *doing the work*. If you are unable to devote fifteen minutes every day to revisit these principles, then commit yourself to focus on one principle every week.

Here is my final suggestion to get you started on the path toward your true destiny. Write, or type a *covenant* with yourself. It should look something like this:

I hereby agree and commit to:

- decide what I really want out of life and act accordingly;

- prepare and work hard to achieve my goals;

- always be true to myself, even if it makes me uncomfortable initially;

- take total responsibility for my life, making no excuses for failures/ shortfalls;

- speak up when I have something to say;

- be creative in my thinking and do not be afraid to look within myself for answers;

- live and work such that my integrity or work ethic is never in question;

- be steadfast in my values and beliefs, even when faced with Goliath opposition;

- never abandon my dreams and passions, no matter how long my pursuit takes;

- believe in myself and know my intention before I start any undertaking;

- agree to disagree with others, and move forward;

- laugh at myself and admit it's okay to be wrong;

- accomplish something outside my normal routine;

- take thirty minutes a day for myself, and in that time remind myself, my actions are what shape my destiny.

I have tremendous respect for all who invested the time to read these principles and took this first step toward self-development. Now, move forward to the next step: *take action* with your acquired knowledge! If you chose only to read this information, then you have only discovered *potential.* If you *act* on this information, you can live with power and purpose.

It is my sincere desire to provoke you to analyze your life, and to think deeply about who you are, and what you desire from life. Your true destiny can only be reached through the authentic you. No matter what, be true to yourself. I would like to end with my favorite quote on success by fourth century philosopher St. Augustine: *"People travel to wonder at the height of the mountains, at the huge waves of the seas, at the long course of the rivers, at the vast compass of the ocean, at the circular motion of the stars, and yet they pass by themselves without wondering."*

Never forget, you are a great wonder. What you accomplish in life is entirely up to YOU! To every man or woman who has abandoned a dream, I encourage you to go back, dust it off, and pursue it again.

Choose what you love and love what you do! Take care of yourself and stay focused on your dreams.

Know who you are, or you might try to be someone else.

—Vincent T. Williams

Life's Toolbox of Clues

In this box are clues left behind by those who exemplified a discovered destiny by their level of achievement. These clues are tools which may be used for many different circumstances. Carry this toolbox with you on life's journey, as a skilled craftsman carries his or her utensils to perform a perfect job.

- Trust in God—Faith is theory, but trust is practical application.

- Stay true to yourself!

- Believe in you and your abilities.

- Visualize the accomplishment of your dreams.

- Never, ever abandon your dreams.

- Always be open-minded about a new or different perspective.

- READ—Read anything that will move you closer to your goals.

- INVEST IN YOURSELF—Buy anything that will move you closer to your goals (seminars, books, workshops).

- Motivation is that which resides within, not something that someone gives you.

- Stay focused on your outstanding goals.

- Do what you love—love what you do.

- Be totally committed to your dreams.

- Live your own dream, not the American Dream.

- BEWARE—Your family and friends are not likely to support you in an uncommon career path, or a path that is not familiar to them.

- When you are not getting the results you want, change your behavior.

- Neither knowledge nor wisdom gives you power; the only one thing that gives you power is action.

- When we change our behavior and take determined action for our dreams, we realize our true destiny.

- If you change your thoughts, you change your life.

- A common trait among high achievers is their insatiable appetite for new knowledge.

- An egotistic condition is a dangerous psychological state—it can create a toxic and potentially lethal flaw in your character and decision making.

- You are designing your life with each moment through the choices you make.

- What happens to us is not as important as how we respond to what happens to us.

- Acquire the self-discipline needed for delayed gratification.

- If you are not failing, you are not trying.

- Leverage the power of your mind to choose how you behave under any circumstance.

- God is the greatest influential source in our lives. Second to his grace, the thoughts we think have the foremost influence on what we will do or become.

- Every person who has achieved anything in life decided to take responsibility for making it happen.

- Your "should-dos" have to become your "must-dos."

- You can alter your present condition by making a conscious commitment to step into the driver's seat.

- It is not important where we start in life; it's how we finish that counts.

- The ability to dream, to see the obstacles, then transform the obstacles into strategies is the distinguishing feature of people who transform the world, rather than just living their lives responding to the world.

Tenets of the Good Book

Even so faith, if it hath not works, is dead, being alone. (James, 2:17 KJV)

And be not conformed of this world: but be ye transformed by the renewing of your mind, that ye may prove what is that good, and acceptable, and perfect will of God. (Romans 12:2 KJV)

Where there is no vision, the people will perish: but he that keepeth the law, happy is he. (Proverbs 29:18 KJV)

Be strong and of good courage: for unto this people shalt thou divide for an inheritance the land, which I sware unto fathers to give them. (Joshua 1:6 KJV)

For as he thinketh in his heart, so is he: Eat and drink, saith he to thee; but his heart is not with thee. (Proverbs 23:7 KJV)

I returned, and saw under the sun, that the race is not to the swift, nor the battle to the strong, neither yet bread to the wise, nor yet riches to men of understanding, nor favour to men of skill; but time and chance happeneth to them all. (Ecclesiastes 9:11 KJV)

A bishop then must be blameless, the husband of one wife, vigilant, sober, of good behaviour, given to hospitality, apt to teach; Not given to wine, no striker, not greedy of filthy lucre; but patient, not a

brawler, not covetous ... (1Timothy 3: KJV)

Delight thyself also in the LORD: and he shall give thee the desires of thine heart. (Psalm 37:4 KJV)

Thou shalt not avenge, nor bear any grudge against the children of thy people, but thou shalt love thy neighbour as thyself: I am the LORD. (Leviticus 19:18 KJV)

Therefore all things whatsoever ye would that men should do to you, do ye even so to them: for this is the law and the prophets. (Matthew 7:12 KJV)

The God of my rock; in him will I trust: he is my shield, and the horn of my salvation, my high tower, and my refuge, my saviour; thou savest me from violence. (2 Samuel 22:3 KJV)

Defining Qualities
and Characteristics
for Consistent Achievement

Purpose: intent—proposed as an aim to oneself; the reason for which something exists.

Responsibility: the state of being accountable, obligated, reliable, and dependable or responsible for the outcome, 'mediocre or fabulous.'

Self-Control: the ability to manage one's emotions and impulses.

Consistency: having reliability and uniformity of successive results.

Discipline: the will to successfully focus and follow a state of order based on submission to rules or a systematic method to obtain a certain result.

Fear: an emotion of apprehension, creating false images of failure prior to the pursuit of your ambitions.

Failure: the condition or fact of not achieving the desired end.

Mental Toughness: emotional resilience of convictions and outlook; not easily influenced or diverted by sentiment or impediments.

Leadership: the ability to guide or show the way; a means of bringing something to a particular condition or result.

Inner-Peace: a state of being free of contention psychologically and spiritually; an arrival at tranquility, self-acceptance, and contentment in spirit, mind, body, and heart.

Destiny: the purpose or future, as arranged or foreordained by the Divine or by God.

Faith: a secure belief in God and a trusting acceptance in God's will.

Wisdom: the right use of information or the capacity to apply knowledge effectively.

Tool: a device, person or something use to facilitate manual or mechanical work or to perform one's occupation or profession.

Strategy: a systematic plan of action designed to achieve a particular goal.

Principles: are external natural laws; a rule or standard; a predetermined mode of action or guide, especially of positive behavior.

Values: are internal and subjective standards, feelings, regard, esteem, worth in usefulness or importance to the individual or possessor.

Mental Outlook: a psychological attitude, perspective, view, or picture that determines how you interpret and respond to life.

Positive Attitude: the mental disposition to see people and situations from an optimistic point of view.

Goal: the plan by which the purpose is intended to achieve.

Vision: the capacity to see beyond one's natural sight.

Visualization: a hypothetical mental simulation of images or visual perception, which enables one to foresee one's achieved goal prior to the pursuit.

Courage: a brave will to press forward in the presence of fear; a daring management of uncertainty.

Perseverance: the power to endure failure and difficulty again and again, motivated by faith in a purpose.

Alignment: to be placed in, or come into, precise adjustment, correct relative position or compatibility.

Determination: a firm or fixed intention to achieve a desired end or destiny.

Humility: the state or quality of being free of pride and arrogance.

Integrity: true character; consistency in one's words and actions; trustworthiness.

Friendship: the capacity to welcome and embrace others unconditionally.

Resilience: the capacity to bounce back when problems arise.

Creativity: an ability to see solutions and fix problems.

Initiative: the ability to discern what needs to be done and take action.

Flexibility: not afraid to change; fluid; flows with growth.

Track Record: experience and success in previous situations.

Self-Efficacy: belief and confidence in one's own ability to accomplish one's desired ambitions.

Executive Ability: the ability to effectively lead and execute large, intricate projects; get things done.

Passion-Directed Life: a chosen path for life, personal or professional, guided by the passion of your heart.

Teachable Moment: a lesson, or education on life possibilities, demonstrated by example, in specific for skeptics.

Magnetic Affect: whereby help comes to those who help themselves, or those working with a purposeful direction; inspired by significance for life.

Big-Picture View: able to see beyond one's own advantage and visualize the overall benefit for others.

Passion: a deeply set emotion of love and desire, which drives you with enthusiasm and zeal to a specific cause or interest. Passion, at times, is felt as a suffering and agonizing desire. Passion is an internal motivator and affords its own reward for the seeker. Passion is insatiable and cannot be extinguished in the face of adversity or upon consumption. Passion guides and guards your decisions and directions. Passion creates the pathway to your destiny!

A Letter to You

Dear Reader,

Prior to publishing this book, I spent some time wandering through my favorite book stores. Of course there were many different literary categories but, in particular, under the self-help and personal development section, it seemed there were thousands of books. I became dizzy, attempting to peruse the countless titles and authors. We choose the books we read for a number of reasons. Yet, sometimes books choose us. It is not by mistake you hold this book in your hand, and I am grateful you found the interest to read it.

Each one of us has different ways to manage our time for reading. Some of us read while waiting for our children during soccer or football practice. To make good use of down time, others read in the lobby of the auto service department or airport boarding area while waiting to catch a flight. How you manage your time to read and what you enjoy reading is important. But as an empowerment author, it is vital that my message rewards you quality and valuable reading. I trust, in reading this book, you were granted a provocative getaway from the daily rat race of your busy life, and replaced your routines with some exploratory and analytical conversation on common-sense, but powerful principles.

I am an everyday common, old-fashion Southern gentleman. I was raised to believe in God and myself. My faith in God endows me a worry free life. However, I am bothered by both wasted talent and unrealized potential. I'm troubled, when I witness individuals with great ability, yet no passion. I am deeply concerned when I witness an entire family unaware they have been infected with a mind-set and spirit of average. I've witnessed both all out living and regretful death. I've been the main character in both a circle *of failure and success. Mainly it's been the ring of success, not because of wealth, but largely because, I've lived my life being true to myself. With my family as my witness, I have always pursued that which is in my heart.*

Growing up in the small town of Mobile, I always had a desire to meet great famous achievers, not to get autographs, just to talk with them. Now, every day, I meet interesting accomplished individuals. Many of my lifelong friendships have stemmed from these rich conversations. I enjoy meeting people, and discussing their guiding principles and philosophies of life. I am always curious to know when and how people know what they want to do in life.

Two things I really enjoy are eating and talking. Down south, we loved to pass time talking on the porch after a good home cooked meal. So, if you have a group, organization, or a book club that plans to read this book, please let me know. I would be delighted to talk with your group about, "How Do I Reach My True Destiny," while eating some good food. I would love to hear the thoughts of your associates as well. Feedback is always help-ful and can be fun. If you have questions or you just want to drop me a line, please do so. Whatever your reason, I can be reached via e-mail at vincewil@williamsgroupinc.com.

It is my sincere wish that you find your true passion in life and that you find a way to pursue it. But before I go, I would like to ask you an impor-tant question. What would you attempt to do with your life, if you knew you could not fail? Have a great day! Do something fun …

Design Your Destiny,

Vincent T. Williams
"Coach"

About This Book

Every human being desires a destiny that characterizes him or her as a success. Even if not conventional, everyone envisions a certain lifestyle. Every thought, decision and action either moves you closer to or away from the success and lifestyle you imagine. With each moment and with each choice, we custom design our destiny. Everything we do counts. The good news is great personal success is possible for every individual, because success is as unique as our fingerprints. No two people will have the identical description of success. But to reach your true destiny, you have to know what it means to you.

In this interactive, action-oriented book, Vincent Williams brings a call to *personal awareness*. He offers a fresh, honest perspective on living and conducting an ongoing investigation of truth; the truth about who you really are. In *How Do I Reach My True Destiny*, Mr. Williams articulates how our environmental and cultural traditions confine our clarity of direction and the ability to take action. He challenges you to find the root cause of that which stifles you and guides you through a process of identifying your inherent gifts and talents. Williams argues that everyone is endowed with specific strengths, and from these, flow the richest opportunities to design a life of passion and true fulfillment.

Mr. Williams reveals the clues and success secrets left behind by those who exemplified a sense of discovered destiny in their accomplishments. In this work, he conveys the principles and strategies of peak performers, champions, and Olympic athletes, from Abraham Lincoln to Ervin "Magic" Johnson, Joe Frazier, Clara "Mother Hale" Hale, Nelson Mandela, and Agnes "Mother Teresa" Gonxhe Bojaxhiu. These individuals symbolize a rich spirit of courage and a strong belief in a set of values used to design their destiny.

You will learn how to:

- Develop a self-image that caters to your inner-distinction

- Acknowledge those dreams and passions deep within

- Devise and implement a plan to achieve your mega-goals

- Effectively manage failures, obstacles and unforeseen challenges

- Discover your unique ability

- Obtain clarity of direction

Filled with strategies and principles of legendary achievers, *How Do I Reach My True Destiny* is life's toolbox; a fortune of wisdom and knowledge, which can only be acquired from those that have gone before us to reach their true destiny. It is the perfect gift.

Vincent T. Williams *"Coach"* is an empowerment speaker/facilitator and author. He resides in Charlotte, North Carolina.

About Vince Williams

Vincent Williams is an everyday, common individual, who has always believed in God and himself. He grew up as a southern gentleman in the deep south of Mobile, Alabama. Convinced that life circumstances are but learning experiences, he lives by a simple philosophy—that self-knowledge grows as you subject yourself to self-examination, listening to your own thoughts, and looking at your own actions; to improve your effectiveness.

Mr. Williams is President/CEO of Williams Group, Inc., training and consulting firm, based in Charlotte, North Carolina. As a professional lecture and facilitator, he has addressed audience nationwide, assisting individuals and organizations with peak performance. His clients have included University of North Carolina Charlotte, Johnson C. Smith University, United Logistics Corporation, the YMCA of The Greater Carolinas, and a host of public schools across the United States.

Prior to forming the Williams Group, Mr. Williams was employed with IBM for seven years. His exemplary performance led to several leadership positions in the areas of Quality Control and Customer Relations. A demonstrated leader, he chaired an Excellence Quality Team which received the Malcolm Baldridge Award of Quality. He was also recognized for leading an Excellence Morale team, which raised the employee morale index of IBM Charlotte employees from the lowest to highest in the nation.

Mr. Williams was founder, President and CEO of ToDay Courier Service, Inc. for nearly 10 years. The company was noted for its outstanding, no-nonsense customer service, maintaining a national client base including Lance Snack Co., Wachovia Bank, Office Depot, and Lockheed Martin Corporation. In addition, Williams is skilled in sports motivational psychology. He was voted Coach of The Year in 1996 and 2002 and he owns the 1998 Charlotte NBA Pro-Am Summer League Championship Title. He is an advocate of social responsibility to humanity and has a strong belief in mentorship. Mr. Williams has been dedicated to a 13-year mentoring relationship with 5 young men in his community.

His affiliations include past and present service on the Life Enrichment Network Board of Directors, Dowd YMCA Board of Managers, Dowd YMCA Volunteer Development Committee-Chair, Dowd YMCA Angel Tree Project Committee, Parks & Recreational Board of Advisors (Mecklenburg County), United Way Campaign Loaned Executive, United Way Allocation Panel, Charlotte Civic League—Treasurer, and Toast Masters of Charlotte.

Vince Williams (Focus)

Mr. Williams is a thought-provoking, enthusiastic, passionate speaker and facilitator. He has been a consultant to church organizations, educators, and college students as well as college and professional athletes. The Williams Group addresses a variety of areas in human, social, and spiritual-development.

The focus of his message is twofold. Foremost, self-actualization—the art of being true to oneself—is essential for personal development. His mantra is '*Follow Your Passion.*' Secondly, Mr. Williams believes maximizing one's individual potential requires a mental transformation from the model posed by Western society which suggests that financial and material gain determines success, to living by the principle of a passion-directed life.

Mr. Williams shares the tools, strategies, and achievement principles of champions and peak performers. He is recognized for his contagious, down to earth personality, which enables him to personally connect with audiences. In his seminars, he shares stories of failure, self-doubt, extreme adversity, determination, and success. His message inspires, but more importantly, it provides a blueprint for a life of achievement.

Vincent Williams is available for organizational conferences, banquets, and benefits.
The Williams Group offers personal coaching for personal and professional development areas of your life.
For more information, call us today at 704-405-7076 or go to
www.vincewilliams.net.

PRESENTATIONS

Workshops—Seminars—Lectures
By
Vincent T. Williams

True Destiny

Fashioned after the book, *How Do I Reach My True Destiny?* This empowering inspirational seminar is designed to guide you toward clarity, authenticity, and true fulfillment in your personal and professional life. This presentation highlights common environmental and cultural impediments which mentally imprison our ability to take action toward fulfilling our deepest desires. You will receive instruction on applying powerful principles when facing barriers to success such as lack of clarity, self-doubt, fear, pessimism, and cynicism.

For more information, or to book a presentation, please contact:

Vincent T. Williams
@
The Williams Group
PO Box 31544
Charlotte, N.C., 28231
e-mail: vincewil@williamsgroupinc.com
Off. 704-405-7076
Fax 704-358-8008
www.mytruedestiny.com

978-0-595-42679-9
0-595-42679-4

Printed in the United States
95911LV00005BA/197/A

9 780595 426799